BOOKS BY

REYNOLDS PRICE

EARLY DARK

REYNOLDS PRICE

EARLY DARK

A PLAY

NEW YORK

ATHENEUM

1977

PS
3566
R54
E3
1977

Library of Congress Cataloging in Publication Data

Price, Reynolds, 1933–
    Early dark.

    I. Title.
PS3566.R54E3   1977   812'.5'4   77–3189
ISBN 0–689–10799–4

FOR

KATHLEEN & HARRY FORD

PREFACE

This play shares plot with a novel called A *Long and Happy Life,* which tells an earlier version of similar events in the lives of a few Americans in the summer, fall, and winter of 1957. The playwright shares the novelist's name and some of his physical and mental traits. He is changed however, by nineteen years.

Thus the play is not the novel dramatized. It is rather the same general set of actions, the same few people seen by a different man who stands elsewhere and sees otherwise. The story of the play differs therefore from the novel's as two alert but separate witnesses' versions of a complex event will inevitably and instructively differ. Comparisons may be made and one version may ultimately prove more useful; but whatever their effects and fates, both stories were told in need and pleasure, in the hope they would cause need and pleasure in others—needs not satisfied by stories alone, whatever their forms.

The story occurs in Warren County in northeastern North Carolina; but while that scene has shaped the people, it has not deformed them; and its characteristics should not be exploited for quaintness or humor, color or patronage. Such people could tell Sophocles or Beckett numerous complicated facts and possibilities.

Stage-Southern accents, gestures, and clothing should be avoided or powerfully restrained. The South is larger than—and linguistically as various as—New England, the MidAtlantic, and a large piece of the Midwest combined. There are almost as many Southern accents as Southerners; and in nearly forty years of play- and moviegoing, I have never heard a non-Southern actor produce one with more than modest accuracy (decamped Southerners frequently offer grievous parodies). A generally non-urban American accent and rhythm is recommended when the play is produced outside its native county.

The clothes are those of upper working-class America of the early 50s (fashion taking a few years then to work its way South).

Any music would derive from church or popular radio—no straight hair and dulcimers. Pervasive country sounds would help—the steady chorus of birds, crickets, frogs till October silence. Vehicle sounds should be carefully controlled; motorcycle noise should be barely indicated if used at all.

Fluidity of progress should be the first aim of set design. There should be a minimum of pauses (within acts only five pauses are implied, and skill might eliminate several of those; scene numbers indicate substantial shifts of time or place). Three physical areas appear necessary, in my mind at least—stage left, the Mustian house (two rooms required, Rosacoke's upstairs); a central all-purpose out-of-doors; and stage right, all other places (the two churches, Mary's, Wesley's, Mr. Isaac's; the lake can lie behind the audience, aisles being used for running swimmers—and in Act Three for the pageant processions). There may be more effective solutions, but a slow set will be bad.

The two church services—black funeral, white pageant—are main supports to the arc of the action: the chief opportunities for ritual expression by different but inextricable races. They must be staged in their urgent solemnity, dignity, and fervor. Costumes for the pageant are simple oddments from family closets, none comic. A touch of condescension will poison both rites and hide the burning target of these lives.

The play can be shown in many right ways. The only wrong way would start by forgetting that the story of the species is mostly lived out in huts, houses, woods, fields—far from towns and cities. These people move with the weight of that certainty, the tragic glee of the well-informed.

R. P. *February 1977*

CHARACTERS

WHITE

EMMA MUSTIAN—*a widow, 45, housekeeper for her children*

MILO—*Emma's son, 24, a tobacco farmer*

RATO—*Emma's son, 22, an Army corporal*

ROSACOKE—*Emma's daughter, 20, a telephone operator. Burdened by vision and intelligence but the credible object of a young man's care*

BABY SISTER—*Emma's daughter, 11, a sixth-grade student*

SISSIE—*Milo's wife, 22, idle*

WESLEY BEAVERS—*local boy, 22, a cycle salesman. Magnetic in stillness, with the air of power abiding its time*

WILLIE DUKE AYCOCK—*local girl, 22, a beautician*

MACEY GUPTON—*local farmer, 25*

MARISE—*Macey's wife and mother of three, 24*

ISAAC ALSTON—*local landowner, 86, half-paralyzed*

MR. MASON—*proprietor of Mason's Lake, a Free Will Baptist preacher, 48*

HEYWOOD BETTS—*scrap-metal merchant from Newport News, Va., 34*

REV. VEREEN—*of Delight Baptist Church, young to middle-aged (unseen)*

DR. SLEDGE—*local physician, 60 (silent)*
SHEPHERDS—*three to five adolescent boys (silent)*
CHOIR—*three to four male and/or female voices*

BLACK

MRS. RANSOM—*Sammy Ransom's mother, 46, a church leader*

REV. MINGIE—*of Mount Moriah Church, middle-aged to old*

MARY SUTTON—*dead Mildred's mother, 37, an occasional housemaid*

SAMMY RANSOM—*Mr. Isaac Alston's man, 22*

ACT ONE

1

Warren County, North Carolina; a small tobacco farm; a Sunday morning in late July 1957. On a downstairs porch of the Mustian home, BABY SISTER, SISSIE, *and* MILO *wait hot and dark. In an upstairs bedroom* EMMA MUSTIAN *sits dressed on the bed. Her daughter* ROSACOKE *faces the window, wearing only her white slip.*

EMMA

Why?

ROSACOKE

He's what I want.

EMMA

Why?

ROSACOKE

He's always been.

EMMA

The world's full of people—

ROSACOKE

Not for me.

EMMA

Since when?

ROSACOKE

(*Still at the window, facing out; realizing as she goes*)
Seven years this November. You had punished me for
laughing that morning in church, and I wanted to die—
which was nothing unusual—but guessed I could live
if I breathed a little air, so I picked up a bucket and
walked to the woods to hunt some nuts and win you
back. It was getting on late. I was hoping you were
worried. I was past Mr. Isaac's in the really deep woods.
The leaves were all gone, but I hadn't found a nut. Still
I knew of one tree Mildred Sutton had showed me—I
was headed for that—and I found it finally. It was
loaded—pecans the size of sparrows—and in the top
fork a boy, a stranger to me. I was not even scared. He
seemed to live there, twenty yards off the ground, staring out dead-level. I said, "Are you strong enough to
shake your tree?" —"If I wanted to," he said. I said,
"Well, want to please; I'm standing here hungry." He
thought and then braced his long legs and arms and
rocked four times—pecans nearly killed me. I rum-
maged round and filled my bucket, my pockets. He had
still not faced me; so I said, "Don't you want to share
some of my pecans?" Then he looked down and smiled
and said, "I heard they were God's." I said, "No, really
they belong to Mr. Isaac Alston. He can't see this far."
—"I can see him," he said. "You may can see Philadelphia," I said—he was looking back north—and he

nodded to that but didn't look down. "How old are you?" I said. He said "Fifteen" and shut up again. "I'm thirteen," I said. He said "You'll live" and smiled once more toward Philadelphia and I came on home. I wanted him then and every day since.

EMMA

You're saying that's a reason to ruin your day?

ROSACOKE

Yes ma'm—my life.

MILO *steps from the porch to the yard, looks up, speaks to* ROSA's *window.*

MILO

You're a fool and you know it. Just as well lie there and wait for snow. (EMMA *starts downstairs*) You'd think Wesley Beavers was General MacArthur—everybody waiting in July sun while he decides to come or stay. What the hell did he say anyhow?

BABY SISTER

Nothing as usual. His mother called Rosacoke Friday night, said Wesley was being discharged on Saturday and would be here to see her by Saturday night.

MILO

Yeah. Well, this is Sunday and the picnic is melting. Rosa, haul your simple self down here!

EMMA

(*In the door*) Milo, hush. What have you ever waited on in your life for more than two minutes?

MILO

I've been waiting six months for my baby boy.

SISSIE

It's half my baby and it may be a girl.

MILO

We've all been waiting—what is it? three years—for Wesley to sail home for good from the Navy and put a smile back on Weeping Willow's face. Last call, Rosa!

EMMA

I told you to hush. She's dressing now. Didn't you hear her walking past midnight, staring at the road?

MILO

No, I sleep when it's dark. Well, I mostly sleep. (*Grins toward* SISSIE)

SISSIE

Are we leaving now and stirring a breeze or am I getting sick?

BABY SISTER

Me too.

EMMA

Be ashamed, all of you. Just shut up and wait. If that girl turned against any one of you, you'd lose your best friend. (*Looks to* ROSA's *window*) Rosa, listen to reason. He'll come in good time—he grew up here; he'll track you down. He doesn't run his own life; show him you run yours. (*Listens for an answer*) Are you coming, Rosa?

ROSACOKE

I'm coming.

MILO

Praise Jesus! Her Highness is going to favor us, huh?

EMMA

Your sister is coming if that's what you mean; and if you speak one hard word to her now, you can leave my house. It's mine till I die.

They are stopped by the distant roar of a motorcycle.

SISSIE

Is this it?

BABY SISTER

Who else?

ROSA *appears at her window unsmiling; then quickly pulls inward as the roar increases, stops,* WESLEY *enters —white shirt, khaki trousers, plain brown shoes. No one greets him.*

WESLEY

All you need to say is "Welcome back to freedom." (*Silence still so he turns to* MILO) You never spent three years in a sailor suit, so you don't know how happy I am.

MILO

I've spent nineteen years staring up a mule's ass. I've spent three years watching my next sister wait around for you. We've all spent this morning watching her wait—and last night too. It's held us up from the church picnic, and Rosacoke all but missed the funeral.

WESLEY

What funeral, Mrs. Mustian?

EMMA

Mildred Sutton died Friday. Colored Mildred, Mary's child—you remember Mildred.

MILO

Having somebody's baby, some unknown father.

EMMA

Rosa grew up with Mildred and kept up with her. Still she was ready to miss Mildred's funeral because of you.

WESLEY

I never heard a word about a death. I got my discharge noon yesterday and have come one hundred and thirty miles, not stopping, this morning to see Rosacoke—haven't even been home. That's the best I could do.

MILO

Noon yesterday was a whole day ago. Where you been so long?

WESLEY

Settling things.

MILO

What waters were troubled? Who you been stirring up?

EMMA

Milo, put this food—and Sissie—in the car. They're cooking too fast. (*Turns to* WESLEY, *yielding now, though* MILO *doesn't move*) Well, you're back home now. We can all make adjustments.

WESLEY

Just today and tonight.

EMMA

Where then?

WESLEY

Back to Norfolk in the morning. Got a good job in Norfolk, selling motorcycles. I'm here to see Rosa.

EMMA

That's news to us. We thought you'd be back here farming for your father.

WESLEY

No ma'm. I decided my chance is in Norfolk.

EMMA

I'm sorry, Wesley. I know your mother's sorry.

WESLEY *smiles and nods,*

MILO

Sorry?—for what? That this boy here is running off again? We all ought to thank the good old Lord—ought to fall on our knees right now and say, "Thank you, Lord, for sparing our family by taking this trouble-maker out of our midst. Now give us some sleep."

WESLEY

Don't thank Him too soon. Norfolk's not round the world.

ROSA *stands at the front door in white, a wide summer hat; walks to the porch steps and smiles down at* WESLEY. *He smiles in reply; quickly finds a harmonica; and plays "Home, Sweet Home," double-time. She advances as he plays, stops three yards away.*

MILO

A motorcycle and a harp—what else? What you bring Rosacoke? What you bring me?

WESLEY

(*Bowing at the waist, hand on his heart; rising with a smile for* ROSA) My actual self. No—(*To* MILO, *shaking his harmonica*) I took a few lessons on this from a friend.

MILO

I'm sure you took all grades of lessons, day-school and night-school. Just don't be teaching my sister your lessons. See what I mean?—I been teaching Sissie. (*Pats* SISSIE's *belly*) Ain't she a good learner? (*Mock-whisper to* SISSIE) At least it hasn't gone to your head, Dollbaby.

SISSIE

Milo, I said I was sick as a dog. Let's roll this car to that damned picnic and find some shade.

MILO

Calm down, Sugar. Take a lesson from Rosa. She turned a new leaf time she heard that cycle.

EMMA

Sissie's right—we've got to get started. Wesley, are you coming to the picnic with us?

WESLEY

If you've got plenty food.

MILO

We could feed the five thousand. But how about you taking Rosa to the funeral? Then you two come on to the picnic together.

WESLEY

I'm not dressed.

MILO

It's a nigger funeral.

EMMA

Milo, Rosa's not well. She can't go bumping through the dust today.

MILO

Of course she can—can't you, Rosa? Sure thing. Put your hat in the saddlebags and, Wesley, go slow. Be a lovely ride. Rosa's first time. First time for everything, Rosa. Come on!

ROSA *takes off her hat and moves toward* MILO. *He snatches at* WESLEY, *pulls his sailor cap off, jams it down on* ROSA's *head.*

MILO

She's in service now!

ROSA *accepts it all, having reached* WESLEY, *though they haven't touched.*

EMMA
Go easy, Milo. Everybody's not brass.

MILO
Not only going easy—I'm spreading joy.

ROSA *moves to leave.* WESLEY *watches a moment, then follows her off.*

MILO
See you at the lake. (*Cycle fires, starts*) You got to pull your dress up!

No one waves. The cycle leaves. EMMA *watches after everyone else has moved toward the car.*

2

An hour later, Mount Moriah Church, a coffin on trestles, piano music. MRS. RANSOM *stands.*

MRS. RANSOM

It is now my duty to read the obituary over this child we all knew and cherished. Miss Mildred Sutton was born in 1936 in the bed where she died. Her mother is Mary Sutton of this community; and her father was Wallace Sutton, now gone. She grew up round here and worked in tobacco for Mr. Isaac Alston and went to school till she started cooking for the Drakes and tending their children that she loved like they were hers. They are at the beach now or would surely be here. Mildred hoped to go with them right to the last and then wasn't able. She stayed here and died on her twenty-first birthday. Her favorite song was "Annie Laurie," which she learned from Miss Rosacoke Mustian who is with us today, representing Mildred's many white friends; and I welcome her here on behalf of the family in their hour of need. I will sing the song now to remember Mildred. (*Lifts her head and begins, no accompaniment*)

"Maxwellton's braes are bonnie where early falls the
    dew;
And 'twas there that Annie Laurie gave me her
    promise true,
 Gave me her promise true which ne'er forgot would
    be;
And for bonnie Annie Laurie I'd lay me doun and
    dee."

MRS. RANSOM *sits.* SAMMY RANSOM *and* REV. MINGIE *rise,
lift the coffin lid.*

REV. MINGIE

Miss Rosacoke, please view Mildred now.

ROSACOKE

Now?

REV. MINGIE

She's ready now.

Piano starts softly. ROSA *stands, comes forward slowly,
looks down at the body.*

MARY

Testify. Testify for Mildred, Rosacoke.

*Voices say "Yes—testify—Amen." Soft music continues.
Wesley's cycle fires and starts, though it doesn't move.*

ROSACOKE

I hadn't seen much of Mildred lately, but we always
observed each other's birthday; and the other evening

I said to myself, "It's Mildred's twenty-first birthday; I should find her," so I walked down to her place after supper and nobody was there but the turkey—(*A child's high voice laughs two notes; the cycle roars, then idles.* ROSA *offers the rest to* MARY) See, I didn't know till the next afternoon you had carried her off. There I was just wanting to give her a pair of stockings and wish her a long and happy life, and she was already gone.

The cycle leaves—slowly through the churchyard, pauses, swells, then rapidly fades. ROSA *shakes her head to* MARY, *stands another moment, half-runs out.*

MARY

Sammy, go help her.

SAMMY RANSOM *rises from beside* MR. ISAAC ALSTON *and follows* ROSA *out. She stands in the churchyard, staring at the road.* SAMMY *stops on the top step.* ROSA *hears him and turns.*

ROSACOKE

Aren't you frying in all that wool?

SAMMY

I'm all right. What's wrong, Rosacoke?

ROSACOKE

(*Pauses, then knows*) Everybody I know is gone. (*Tears come silently*)

SAMMY

I'm here; you know me. And if you're needing to go somewhere, Sammy can take you.

ROSACOKE

Place I need to go is too long a ride for you and Mr. Isaac.

SAMMY

Where's that?

ROSACOKE

The laughing academy. No, thank you, Sammy, but I'm going home and I can walk that.

SAMMY

In this heat today?

ROSACOKE

We've played baseball in worse than this—you and me and Mildred. Sammy, go back. I've ruined things enough without taking you away. Tell Mary I'm sorry.

SAMMY

No telling where Wesley is, Rosacoke, with that machine.

ROSACOKE

No, maybe not but you know I've got to find him.

SAMMY

Good luck then.

ROSACOKE

Same to you. We need it.

She leaves. SAMMY *watches her out of sight.*

3

A half-hour later, a clearing in MR. ISAAC's *woods.* ROSA
*enters, moves toward a spring, kicks off her shoes, tests
the water with a foot.*

ROSACOKE

Alaska! (*Sinks both feet in*) If any of you snakes are
still in there, you can have these feet and welcome to
them! (*Sits awhile, eyes shut, head back, hat beside her.
Then she looks down, draws her dress high on her
thighs, and rubs their smoothness*) White as a fish
belly. Never mind. You're saving it, Honey, till the right
time comes. Whenever that is, whenever that is.
(WESLEY *enters behind her, comes silently forward; and
stands behind her, staring down*) What do you know
about this spring?

WESLEY

I know somebody has stirred hell out of it.

ROSACOKE

That was Rosacoke. Remember her? She was rinsing
her feet; they were badly in need (*Lowers her dress,*

takes her hat, and stands) I don't stir springs up every day, Wesley. I don't strike out for home in the blistering dust every day either; try to plan my life a little better than that.

WESLEY

Ought not to have planned on Wesley then.

ROSACOKE

That may well be.

WESLEY

You ready for this picnic?

ROSACOKE

I'm forgetting that. By the time we got there, they'd all be gone—

WESLEY

Who are they, Rosa? I didn't know we were going to see them.

ROSACOKE

—And you haven't said a word about where you went in the midst of Mildred's funeral, making me look like a barefaced fool.

WESLEY

I went to get something I hope to need, and I never asked you to act like a fool.

ROSACOKE

I can't go looking like the Tarbaby. You'll have to stop at home and let me change.

WESLEY

Clothes aren't what you need. Everybody'll look like Tarbabies by now, hot as it is.

ROSACOKE

I'm not everybody.

WESLEY

I knew that. (*Smiles, extends a hand to her*)

ROSACOKE

(*Holds her separate ground*) Then tell me who you are.

WESLEY

The one standing here. The one that's here to see you. (*Extends the hand again*)

ROSACOKE

How did you find me?

WESLEY

You found me, remember? I was up a tree, peaceful.

ROSACOKE

No, here—now, I mean.

WESLEY

(*Shuts his eyes, draws breath through his nose*) I could find you on the moon.

ROSACOKE

Don't strain your powers. This is North Carolina.

WESLEY

All one place to me—you're in it; I found you.

ROSA *takes his hand finally; they leave together.*

4

Midafternoon, Mason's Lake, Delight Church picnic. EMMA *and* SISSIE *sit in the shade,* MARISE *and* MACEY GUPTON *nearby.* MILO *and* WILLIE DUKE AYCOCK *scramble at water's edge.*

WILLIE
Milo, stop! You're a married man.

WESLEY *and* ROSA *enter and watch.*

MILO
Damn right, I'm married—and love every minute—but you ain't, Honey; and you ain't getting Wesley. He belongs to the Mustians.

EMMA AND SISSIE
Milo!

WILLIE *has struggled free and moves toward the women's bathhouse.*

MILO

Willie, I warned you. Rosa, hold him down—the enemy's approaching.

WILLIE

Hey, Wesley. Hey, Rosa.

ROSACOKE

Hey, Willie.

MILO

(*Rearranging his crotch*) Come on in, Wesley, but stay off that slide. I've ruined myself—don't deprive Rosa of a lovely future.

ROSACOKE

Milo, behave. This is Sunday, remember?

BABY SISTER

(*Runs in*) You missed the baptizing. I've baptized all the Guptons today, some more than once.

WESLEY

Glad you got them before they passed on.

BABY SISTER

You two don't look so good yourselves.

ROSACOKE

Where's Mama?

BABY SISTER

Nursing Sissie yonder in the shade.

WESLEY *moves toward the bathhouse;* ROSA *toward her mother, skirting the lake, taking her time.*

MILO

(*From the lake*) Come on, Rosa. Stand up for your rights!

ROSA *ignores him but quickens her step toward* EMMA, *still fanning a prostrate* SISSIE.

EMMA

Fix your hair, Rosa. You look like you rode in on a circular saw.

ROSACOKE

If that's what you call a motorcycle, I did.

SISSIE

I wish somebody had took me riding on a motorcycle on a rocky road five months ago, and I wouldn't be sick as a dog today.

ROSACOKE

What's wrong with Sissie?

EMMA

Nothing. How was the funeral?

ROSACOKE

Mama, it wasn't a show.

EMMA

I know that. I just thought you might have heard who was father to Mildred's baby.

SISSIE

I'll tell you who the father of this baby is (*Hits her belly a thud;* WESLEY *runs from the bathhouse, calls "Milo," and dives*)—that fool by the slide acting five years old. And if I have anything tamer than a monkey, I'll be a lot luckier than your black friend Mildred.

But ROSA *watches* WESLEY.

EMMA

He can dive all right—Wesley. Can't he?

ROSACOKE

He can do that.

EMMA

They must be trying to touch the bottom. It's twenty-feet deep.

SISSIE

If they're on the bottom, they're eat-up with leeches.

EMMA

Wesley's too speedy for any leech to catch.

ROSACOKE

Amen.

SISSIE

Well, I can't speak for the leeches of course; but Willie Duke Aycock has taken hold.

EMMA

Willie can't keep up with those boys long, can't swim good as a window weight.

SISSIE

No, but she can float—got God's own waterwings in her halter. Remember her winning that Dairy Princess contest?—nearly broke up school for a month: boys laughing.

ROSACOKE

I don't notice Milo swimming away from her.

SISSIE

Milo can swim her to Mesopotamia, but he's on a rope and the end of that rope is anchored right here. (*Pats her belly, smiles*)

EMMA

(*To* ROSA) Consider the source.

ROSACOKE

Yes ma'm, I'll try.

ROSA *wanders off, still watching the lake; approaches the* GUPTONS—MARISE *sitting,* MACEY *and* FREDERICK *asleep.*

MARISE

Don't step on my baby, Rosacoke.

ROSACOKE

I'm sorry. I was watching the swimming, Marise. You been swimming?

*The baby—*FREDERICK—*launches a yell.*

MARISE

Haven't swam since before my first baby. (*Wraps* FREDERICK *tighter in his blanket; his crying grows frantic*)

ROSACOKE

He's roasting.

MARISE

No, he's not. (*Opens her dress, lifts* FREDERICK *to her breast, gently chides him*) Just wait for once.

MILO *and* WESLEY *enter with a kicking* WILLIE *in their arms, dump her like a sack.*

WILLIE

(*To* WESLEY) Child, you have *grown.*

MILO

Drown, Willie. Go on and drown. No demand for you.

WILLIE *stands, abandoned, and enters the bathhouse.*

MACEY

(*Wakened by the skirmish*) Milo's doing his duty for you, Rosa.

ROSACOKE

(*Smiles, embarrassed; looks down to* MARISE) Marise, I'll see you—

MARISE *is lost in her suckling baby;* ROSA *moves again to her mother.* MILO *spots her, runs, picks her up, delivers her at* EMMA'S *feet.* ROSA *fumbles to a dignified posture.* MILO *rummages in* SISSIE'S *bag, finds two cigars, lights both at once.* WESLEY *approaches.*

EMMA

Milo, I asked you once to go easy. Everybody's not as strong as you.

MILO

(*Lays a gentle hand on* ROSA'S *leg*) I don't mean harm.

ROSACOKE

I'll remember that.

EMMA

That leech means harm. (*Points to* WESLEY'S *leg—a leech is fastened to* WESLEY'S *thigh. He picks at it, halts in repulsion, stamps his foot.* ROSA *comes forward on her knees, looks, touches it*) Don't pull it off; he'll bleed to death.

MILO

Leave it alone. It's hungry like me and Wesley won't miss that little drop of blood. Do you good. Cool you down. Ease your pressure.

WESLEY

I can ease my pressure other ways, Milo, than by things on me; and if you're so interested in feeding dumb animals, I'll stick him on you soon as I get him off.

MILO

Take your cigar and burn him off—a gift to celebrate my baby boy.

SISSIE

(*To* MILO) Count your chickens when they chirp.

WESLEY *takes the cigar, tries to touch the leech but slips and burns his thigh. He holds it out to* ROSA.

WESLEY

Do it please.

ROSA *takes the cigar, flicks the ash off neatly, and accurately touches the leech's mouth. It flaps to the ground; she stamps it with her shoe, held in her hand; then she ties* WESLEY'S *wound with a long white handkerchief from her pocket.*

MILO

Thank her, Son. She saved your life.

WESLEY

She knows I thank her.

MILO

Saying is believing.

WESLEY

Thank you.

ROSACOKE

You're welcome.

*They take a silent moment to calm themselves—both
the men lying (*WESLEY *on his stomach*), SISSIE *propped
in her daze,* ROSA *reclining on one elbow, only* EMMA
sitting up. BABY SISTER *wanders up from the lake, also
calmed by fatigue.*

BABY SISTER

Mr. Isaac's come.

SAMMY RANSOM *enters with* MR. ISAAC's *armchair, places
it, leaves, returns with* MR. ISAAC *in his arms, seats him
carefully.*

ROSACOKE

Wonder why he came this far in the sun to sit a few
minutes in that old chair?

MILO

Probably planning to buy the lake—owns everybody
in it.

ROSACOKE

Milo, feed your face and hush. Some people in the
world think of something but money even if you can't.

MILO

I'll think of anything you name, Red Rose, if you'll
make Mr. Isaac pay me all he owes this family—
Granddaddy, Daddy, me: fifty years of chewing dust
in his hard fields so he can pay a trained ape to haul
him round.

ROSACOKE

He went to Mildred's funeral, which few here did.

MILO

Didn't have a choice there—didn't Sammy have to go?

ROSACOKE

Meaning what?

MILO

Meaning that is the nigger killed your friend Mildred by stuffing her guts with a bastard boy and not seeing to her when her time came.

ROSACOKE

You can't prove that.

MILO

No, and Mildred couldn't either. If you back up into an airplane motor, you can't name the one blade slices you first.

EMMA

That's enough, Milo. Joke but don't lie. Mr. Isaac isn't looking for money and you know it. He's living out the end of the life he was handed; you'll have to do the same. You want him to die just because you're young? We've worked for him, sure—it was work or eat gravel— but he's been good to us. The night that truck killed your drunk father, I was sitting in the back room, blind with grief, wondering could I ever feed four helpless children, when I heard a knock and went to the door.

There was Mr. Isaac handing me fifty dollars, folded small as my thumbnail, saying, "Emma, I guess he is far better off."

MILO

Fifty dollars—ummm. (*Kisses air loudly*) Thank you, Mr. Isaac. You saved four lives. Milo worked all those years just because he loved it. Any rest would have ruined him.

EMMA *gathers to answer but* BABY SISTER *sings.*

BABY SISTER

"Praise God from whom all blessings flow.
Praise Him all creatures here below.
Praise Him above ye heavenly host.
Praise Father, Son, and Holy Ghost."

On "Ghost," FREDERICK GUPTON *cries again.*

EMMA

You scared him, Sister, mentioning ghosts.

MILO

All that baby needs is a bust in the mouth.

WESLEY

(*Pushing up with sudden boldness*) —What they all need.

EMMA

Hush.

SISSIE

He's had it twice already since noon.

MILO

Nobody ever gets enough—do they, Wesley? (*Searches a box, finds a chicken leg, eats it*)

WESLEY *doesn't answer but* MACEY GUPTON *rises and comes to* MILO.

MACEY

You people staying on for supper, Milo?

MILO

Yeah, spending the weekend—camping out.

MACEY *accepts the rebuff with a smile, waves, heads back to* MARISE.

EMMA

Don't tell a lie.

MILO

You know he was fishing for an invitation to bring that squad of peeled squirrels over here and eat our stuff.

EMMA

They could have what Rosa and Wesley haven't touched—you children eat something.

ROSA *shakes her head No.*

WESLEY

I'm fine, Mrs. Mustian.

EMMA

You'll both die by dark.

MILO

Leave them be. They got private means of nourishment.

Since MILO's *rebuff, the* GUPTONS *have slowly prepared to leave.* ROSA *has watched with willful attention.* WESLEY *secretly works a hand to her leg.*

WESLEY

Look at me.

ROSACOKE

I'm watching God's beautiful sunset, Wesley—beats any human sight at hand.

WESLEY

Not me. Not you. I've come a long way to see one human. (*Presses her leg again. She will not respond*)

ROSACOKE

Sit still then and look. Stop running and watch.

WESLEY

I was watching when you found me, the first day ever.

ROSACOKE

Not me though, Wesley. You barely saw me.

WESLEY

That's your one opinion. There's at least one more. I've come here today. I'm watching just you.

ROSACOKE

Put your shades on then.

WESLEY *laughs gently, watches.* WILLIE *emerges dressed from the bathhouse, looks toward* WESLEY.

MACEY

Willie, we're ready.

WILLIE

One minute, Macey.

WILLIE *moves toward* WESLEY; BABY SISTER *moans;* MILO *grins toward* ROSA, *about to speak.*

EMMA

Milo, pass me that basket and don't say a word.

MILO *obeys. All watch* WILLIE *pass.*

WILLIE

How're you, Mrs. Mustian? Wesley, can I speak to you?

WESLEY *waits a moment, then flings himself up and follows* WILLIE *four steps from* ROSA. WILLIE *whispers to him; he smiles and shrugs—neither Yes nor No.*

WILLIE

O.K. I'll wait. (*Heads toward the* GUPTONS, *who straggle away*)

WESLEY *slowly moves back to* ROSA, *sits—not lies—in his previous place. Embarrassed moments.*

MILO

How many more?

WESLEY

More what?

MILO

Women trailing you. Bet they're strung up the road clear from here to Norfolk, waiting on you to pass.

No answer from WESLEY.

SISSIE

Milo just wishes he had a few, Wesley.

MILO

How you know I don't have a stable full?

SISSIE

If you do, Sissie's got the key to your stable, Son.

EMMA

You all ought to kneel in the dirt right here and thank God above He doesn't strike you dumb.

MILO

I'm joking, Mama—a little vacation. No need to tune in.

EMMA

I wasn't tuned in. I was thinking how lucky every one of you is—resting and fed. Think of your brother and what he's doing.

MILO

Rato is happy as a coot where he is—all he can eat of that good Army food, making twice as much money as he'd ever make here with the brain he got.

EMMA

I wasn't worried about him eating, and he got all the brain the Lord intended. I was just regretting he missed Mildred's funeral—off in flat Oklahoma, marching for the government on a Sunday hot as this.

ROSACOKE

(*With sudden bitterness*) Why didn't you go then and write him a description?

EMMA

My duty was with my own.

ROSACOKE

Deviling eggs for Milo to choke on?—that what you call your own? And fanning the flies off Sissie's belly? And keeping Baby Sister from drowning the Guptons? I'm glad you're so sure of what's yours and what's not.

EMMA

I don't see why you're acting so grand. You said yourself you didn't stay to the end.

ROSACOKE

No, I didn't. You want to know why? Because Wesley
Beavers wouldn't sit with me in respect to the dead but
stayed in the churchyard, shining that engine; and then
when they called me to witness for Mildred, he cranked
up and tore off and left me and I ran.

MILO

You can't get upset every time Wesley leaves. All us
tomcats got to make our rounds.

ROSACOKE

Milo, you've turned out to be one of the sorriest people
I know.

MILO

Thank you, ma'm. What about your friend Wesley
here?

ROSA *looks to* WESLEY—*the back of his head; he does
not turn.*

ROSACOKE

I don't know about my friend Wesley. I don't know
what he plans one minute to the next. I don't know my
place in that line of women you say is strung waiting
from here to Norfolk.

MILO

Wesley, what is Rosa's place in your string of ladies?
Being her oldest brother, it's my duty to ask.

WESLEY *lies still a moment, then suddenly rolls and faces* ROSA—*staring at her chest as if searching for a number, her place in line. When he opens his mouth to speak, she runs barefoot to the edge of the lake.*

EMMA

What have you done to Rosacoke, Wesley?

WESLEY

Not a thing, Mrs. Mustian. I hadn't said a word.

EMMA

Try saying some then. She's sick on silence.

MILO

It's her battery, Wesley—battery needs charging. You know how to charge up a battery, don't you?

EMMA

The child's had a sadder day than any of you know.

MILO

Sad over what?

EMMA

Mildred's funeral, all *this*—

MILO

No use grieving about that funeral. I knew Mildred as long as Rosa, and Mildred didn't get a thing she didn't ask for—giving herself to any boy that passed. Nothing happens to people that they don't ask for.

EMMA

(*Struggles to her feet, takes the box of supper from* MILO's *lap*) I'm asking you to take me home. That's the sorriest thing you've said in years, and the sun is going down. Mildred Sutton was twenty-one years old and—black, blue, or green—she died in pain. Baby Sister, come help me fold this blanket. (SISSIE, MILO, *and* WESLEY *stand ashamed as* EMMA *and* BABY SISTER *prepare to leave. Ready,* EMMA *moves to* WESLEY; *speaks privately*) Wesley, do you think you can ease that child?

WESLEY

I'll try.

EMMA

And bring her home safe and not abuse her feelings?

WESLEY

Mrs. Mustian, other people have feelings real as hers, which they can't speak.

EMMA

She's forcing us to break her.

WESLEY

I don't want that.

EMMA

She's chosen you for it. Leave her to me, Wesley—here now, clean—or learn how to bear her.

They both wait, looking at ROSA's *back.* WESLEY *turns to* EMMA.

WESLEY

I'm still here, you notice.

EMMA

Can I hold you to that?

WESLEY

If I get any help.

EMMA *nods again, turns.* MILO, SISSIE, *and* BABY SISTER *straggle off.* EMMA *stops at* MR. ISAAC's *chair.*

EMMA

Mr. Isaac, you staying till they drain the lake?

MR. ISAAC

I'm staying till last. I like to be last.

EMMA

Well, you're doing fine at it. You can go now though. Those children don't know you're left in the world. He'll be getting tired, Sammy.

SAMMY

He'll tell me, Mrs. Mustian.

EMMA *touches* MR. ISAAC *on the shoulder and leaves. As the following starts,* MR. ISAAC *signs to* SAMMY, *who walks him off; then returns for the chair.* WESLEY *moves toward* ROSA *slowly in silence, sits behind her, lays one hand across her eyes.*

WESLEY

Who am I?

ROSACOKE

(*At once*) You're Wesley. (*Waits*) That doesn't say why you act the way you do.

WESLEY

Because I'm Wesley. You asked to know Wesley.

ROSACOKE

(*Thinks, nods*) Here comes a breeze.

They savor it a moment; then WESLEY *lays a hand on* ROSA's *knee.*

WESLEY

Let's swim before it's night.

ROSACOKE

What would I swim in?—my lily-white skin? This filthy dress is all I've got.

WESLEY

You could rent one over at the drink stand there.

ROSACOKE

I wouldn't put on a public bathing suit if I never touched water, and I thought you got a bellyful of underwater sports with Willie Duke Aycock.

WESLEY

No.

ROSACOKE

No what?

WESLEY

No, I didn't get a bellyful.

He smiles but she pulls away, repelled again. He sees his error, hopes to mend it, stands, leaves. The sounds of his diving begin. ROSA *watches.* MR. MASON *approaches behind, watches too.*

MR. MASON

Young lady, what kin is that boy to you?

ROSACOKE

No kin. I came with him. We're the scraps of Delight Church picnic is all. He just got out of the Navy—that boy—and he's trying to recall every trick he learned.

MR. MASON

He must be, yes. I wish he wasn't doing it on my time though. I mean I'm a preacher, and I got to go preach, and the law says nobody dives when I ain't watching. He can swim great rings round me, I know; but Delight Church paid me to lifeguard you—so long as he dives, I got to guard.

ROSACOKE

Wesley, Mr. Mason has got to go home.

WESLEY

(*At a distance*) Go easy, Mr. Mason.

MR. MASON

(*Waves, laughs*) Lady, I'm going to leave him alone and deputize you a lifeguard for him. You look strong enough. He's your life to save from here on in. (*Takes out his watch*) It's six-thirty now and I'm preaching in an hour. What must I preach on, Lady?

ROSACOKE

If you don't know by now, I'm glad I haven't got to listen. (*Smiles*)

MR. MASON

What I mean to say is, give me your favorite text; and that's what I'll preach on.

ROSACOKE

(*Thinks briefly*) "Then Jesus asked him what is thy name and he said Legion."

MR. MASON

(*Lost, then at last*) Yes ma'm, that is a humdinger. (*Pauses*) Hope you people enjoyed your day. Come back to see me anytime it's hot. I'm always here; so's the water. (*Goes four steps; turns again to see* WESLEY, *then* ROSA; *speaks with genuine concern*) Take care of him, Lady. He's younger than I thought.

ROSACOKE

Twenty-two years old—been to Spain and France.

MR. MASON

Twenty-two's barely strong enough to walk. Jesus never spoke a sound till he was past thirty.

ROSACOKE

He thought a lot though.

MR. MASON

(*Thinks again, smiles*) You win them all, don't you? Got a fine gift, Lady—confound babes and fools. Just use it right please.

ROSA *nods; he leaves. She turns back toward* WESLEY.

WESLEY

(*Still distant*) Rosa, you got anything I can drink?

ROSACOKE

What you mean?

WESLEY

I mean I'm thirsty.

ROSACOKE

You're standing in several thousand tons of spring water. (*Goes on watching as* WESLEY *approaches, soaked and serious*) The drink stand is closed. We're on our own.

WESLEY *nods, extends a hand to her hair, stops short of a touch, moves off to the bathhouse.* ROSA *thinks they are leaving, goes to find her shoes and hat. She puts on her shoes as* WESLEY *appears in the bathhouse door, having added only a shirt to his trunks.*

ROSACOKE

Who stole your pants?

WESLEY

Rosa, come here.

WESLEY *waves her to him. She goes, takes his proffered hand; and he leads them off on a walk round the lake. After six slow steps and silence from* WESLEY, ROSA *stops.*

ROSACOKE

Aren't we going home? Mr. Mason has shut it; maybe we should go.

WESLEY

Maybe I can find some drinking water.

ROSACOKE

(*Accepting his lead again but with protest*) Wesley, there is water at every gas station between here and home. Why have we got to go tearing through some strange somebody's bushes?

WESLEY

(*Stops*) Please hush, Rosa. (*Strokes her hair*)

ROSACOKE

(*Steps away, touches her hair quickly*) Sun has bleached me till I look like a tramp.

WESLEY

What would you know about a tramp, bleached or black?

ROSACOKE

I know you don't have to go to Norfolk to find one.

WESLEY

What do you mean?

ROSACOKE

You know who I mean.

WESLEY

If it's Willie you mean, she'll be in Norfolk tomorrow morning with all the other tramps you know.

ROSACOKE

What's she going for?

WESLEY

To ease her pain. (*Smiles*) No, she's got a job.

ROSACOKF

Doing what?

WESLEY

Curling hair.

ROSACOKE

What does she know about curling hair with that mess she's got?

WESLEY

I don't know but she's moving up, bag and baggage.

ROSACOKE

What was she asking you about then?

WESLEY

Would I ride her up.

ROSACOKE

On that motorcycle?—a hundred-thirty miles?

WESLEY

Yes.

ROSACOKE

Then she's crazier than even I thought she was. (*Moves two steps away*) Are you taking her?

WESLEY

Don't know yet.

ROSACOKE

When will you know?

WESLEY

Time I'm home tonight.

WESLEY *goes to her, takes her hand again; they walk on farther to trees above the lake.* ROSA *finally pulls at his lead.*

ROSACOKE

We'll both catch terrible poison-oak—which Milo will
laugh at till Christmas at least—and you won't find
any water up here.

WESLEY

Maybe water's not what I'm looking for.

ROSACOKE

I don't notice gold dust lying around—what are you
hunting? (WESLEY *leads her to a large tree and sits
beneath it.* ROSA *holds his hand but doesn't sit*) Night'll
come and catch us here, and we'll get scratched to
pieces stumbling out. (WESLEY *looks up, not smiling;
pulls her hand. She sits beside him and smooths her
hair. He takes her smoothing hand, lifts her hair, and
kisses her neck. She sits upright, eyes open, face clench-
ing.* WESLEY *works on till she pulls away*) How much
else did you learn in the Navy?—harmonica playing,
motorcycle riding, gnawing on girls like sides of meat.
Uncle Sam got his money's worth in you. (WESLEY
sits far back, his face all dark) Wesley, where are you?

WESLEY

I was right there with you. (*Waits*) I'm here, I guess.

ROSACOKE

You guess. You *guess*? Do you guess I'm made out of
brass like Willie to trail behind you and beg for notice?
You guess I can sit on another seven years, wondering
who Wesley is and where Wesley is and is Wesley ever
coming home, calming down, resting long enough to
have him a life? You guess I can live on in mystery like

this till you finally decide to come out of cover and speak your mind?—say "Rosa, I'm ready to carry my share" or "Rosa, get your fool self home to your Mama." All I'm asking you to do is say. Do you guess you love me or that I love you?

WESLEY
(*Waits, still dark; then his voice half-strange*) I've answered that the only way I know how. I'm here by you. (*Moves forward far enough to take light again*)

ROSACOKE
(*Studies him closely*) I love you, Wesley. When I see you, I do. I know this isn't what a girl ought to say; but when you have sat silent seven whole years, waiting for somebody you love to speak and you don't know one reason why you love them or even what you want them to say—then there comes a time when you have to speak. I've spoken and I'm here.

WESLEY
I knew that, Rosa. Wesley is here.

He begins his answer the way he can—gently kissing her eyes, lips, neck; then moving downward. At first she responds, then balks, and stops him with her hand.

ROSACOKE
Is that everything you want out of me?

WESLEY
It's right much, Rosa. (*Waits*) We're not exactly strangers. Listen, if you're thinking of Mildred's trouble,

you'll be all right. It's why I left the funeral— (*Touches his shirt pocket*)

ROSACOKE

(*Stands suddenly*) Take me home please. It's nearly night.

WESLEY

Of course it's night. What the hell you want—floodlights?

ROSACOKE

I said take me home.

WESLEY

You say a lot, Rosa—more than you understand. Try living those words. (*She does not turn so* WESLEY *stands*) You know I'm going to Norfolk tomorrow. You know that, don't you?

ROSACOKE

I know it. (*Moves to leave*)

WESLEY

And that maybe I'm riding Willie up there?

ROSACOKE

You can ride Willie up the seaboard coast, if she's what you want. Just take care she doesn't have Mildred's trouble either.

ROSA *leaves and waits near the bathhouse—full night now.* WESLEY *follows separately, slowly; enters the bath-*

house, comes out with his clothes. Facing ROSA, *three steps away, he slides off his trunks; stands bare before her—to punish and tempt her. Then slowly, still watching her, he dresses. She bears the sight with no visible response.*

WESLEY

You ever know that you really want me—not a dream about me but a person you can see and touch: *not you* —you let me know.

ROSA *nods, moves quickly off.* WESLEY *follows slowly.*

ACT TWO

Amanda: Why is this in other languages?

Me: It's the languages of the countries.

Amanda: Well, it's hard to read.

MiddAction Fair

Raising a Hand for Action....

Tuesday, September 14, 2010
6:00–7:30 P.M. in McCullough Social Space

Network with representatives from organizations specializing in...

Mentoring 🖐 Environment 🖐 Hunger 🖐 Poverty 🖐
Homelessness 🖐 Public Health & **More!**

Sponsored by the Alliance for Civic Engagement Office

1

The Mustian house, a Saturday afternoon in early November, BABY SISTER *sits on the porch in a sweater.* ROSA *enters in a dark winter coat, turns, and waves behind to her unseen driver.*

ROSACOKE
Thank you, Mr. Coleman. I'll see you Monday morning. (*His car drives off*)

BABY SISTER
Hear anything good today?

ROSACOKE
(*Moves slowly up, sits on the steps, thinks, then smiles*) How about this?—I was putting through a call from some man in Vaughan to a woman in Weldon. The first word he said was "Precious, it's *over.*"

BABY SISTER
What did she say?

She waited a minute—I thought I'd broke the circuit—
and then in a voice that would saw baked bricks, she
said, "Little Buddy, that's what *you* think. I air-
conditioned my car for you, and I'm not lying in it out
here by myself!"

BABY SISTER

What else?

ROSACOKE

She hung up. Otherwise, the usual funerals and
wrecks. I'm worn flat out from other people's news.
(*She sits on a moment, eyes shut, leaning back; then
stands to go in—tired but not unhappy. She has
touched the door before* BABY SISTER *speaks*)

BABY SISTER

You can stop waiting now.

ROSACOKE

Was I waiting?

BABY SISTER

Yes.

ROSACOKE

(*Lightly*) For Jesus to call me to heaven and rest. For
my hair to curl by itself in the night—

BABY SISTER

For a letter. You got it. I put it on your mantel. (ROSA
*opens the door and enters, not running but intent as
she climbs to her room.* BABY SISTER *calls behind her*)
You're supposed to say thank you.

ROSACOKE

Thank you.

As ROSA *climbs, her room is lighted.* SISSIE *is there at the window with the letter, straining to read it through the envelope. She is nine-months pregnant.* ROSA *finds her there.*

ROSACOKE

Leave!

SISSIE

I was dusting your things, trying to help.

ROSACOKE

Get out, Sissie.

SISSIE

It's all the doctor will let me do—a little dusting.

ROSACOKE

(*Snatches her letter*) And a little reading? Don't strain your eyes.

SISSIE

Thank you, Miss God-in-Heaven, I won't. (*Moves toward the door, turns*) And neither will you, not reading that—gone more than three months and writes two lines.

ROSACOKE

Sissie Abbott, just don't forget who you are and how you are in this house of ours—catching Milo like you did.

SISSIE

(*Limps out the door, holding chest and belly*) Milo,
help me!

The following is clearly heard from the stairs while ROSA
shuts and locks her door, wipes the letter on her coat,
and opens it.

MILO

Has your time come, Sugar?

SISSIE

I don't know, Milo, and I don't care. I'd be better dead
than bringing children to this house.

MILO

What's wrong now?

SISSIE

I was dusting Rosa's room when she ran in just now
and yelled things to me I wouldn't whisper to a dog.

MILO

Like what?

SISSIE

She said I had no right to be here, that I got you dis-
honest—

MILO

(*Running to* ROSA's *door and knocking*) Rosa, who the
hell do you think you are, abusing Sissie when she's ten
days overdue? You trying to kill her? (*Waits for word;
there is none*) Speak to me—I feed your face.

ROSACOKE

(*Moves to the door but leaves it shut*) You don't. I
work as hard as you.

MILO

I'll trade you then. (ROSA *opens quickly and faces him
gravely*) —You run this farm from now till next fall,
and I'll make long-distance calls for rich folks and
snoop-in on them.

ROSACOKE

(*Thinks, nods, extends the letter*) A deal—start now.
Start by answering this. Everybody else here has read it.
Go on.

MILO

I'll start Monday morning. You keep your own mail.
I'm already married.

SISSIE

(*Unseen*) Milo, please.

MILO

(*Calls toward her gently*) Just get calm now. If the
baby's coming, I'll call Dr. Sledge. If he's not, just rest.
Rest's what we all need.

ROSACOKE

Amen to that.

MILO *gives a little half-apologetic wave and goes downstairs.* ROSA *shuts her door, moves again to her window.*
EMMA *meets* MILO *at the foot of the stairs.*

EMMA

Has Sissie started?

MILO

I doubt it. She was helping out, dusting Rosa's room. Rosa walked in while Sissie was touching a letter from Wesley—nothing to it. (EMMA *nods and at once a great roar starts above*) What the hell is that?

EMMA

An airplane—

They both run to the porch.

MILO

Crashing—or landing hard.

EMMA

In Aycock's field.

SISSIE

(*Inside*) Mi-lo—

MILO

Sugar, hold on. Mama, go sit with Sissie. I better go see how many dead fools we got.

MILO *goes.* EMMA *climbs a few steps, listens.*

EMMA

Sissie, you all right?

SISSIE

(*Unseen*) I can't say now.

EMMA

Then I'll ask you later. (*Waits, looks upward, then climbs to* ROSA *and opens the door*)

ROSACOKE

(*From her bed, half-risen*) Mama, I've begged everybody to knock.

EMMA

Don't make me mad before I can speak. I've climbed fourteen high steps to talk to you.

ROSACOKE

What about?

EMMA

I wanted to show you this old picture I found today. (*Reaches to her pocket for a stiff tan photograph, offers it to* ROSA)

ROSACOKE

(*Still reclining, takes the picture*) Who is it of?

EMMA

I can't place the stout one; the tall one is your father.

ROSACOKE

(*Rises slowly, turns it over*) "Ocean View, Virginia. July 1915." (*Waits, faces* EMMA) I never saw him so clear before.

EMMA

I never knew there was his likeness in the world, except what Milo has got round his eyes; and then I

found this old box of collars. It must have been the
time your grandfather took them to water for the day.
It amounted to the only trip he ever gave them, and it
ended awful because he put a five-dollar bill in his shoe
in case of emergency and then walked ten miles up and
down the sand. About leaving time, emergencies arose—
one was your father wanting a plaster-Paris statue of
Mutt and Jeff—so your grandfather sat down and took
his shoe off; and the money was just little soggy crumbs.
He'd worn it out. He talked about that for thirty years.

ROSACOKE

(*Still studying the picture*) Had you seen him by then?

EMMA

Many times.

ROSACOKE

Did you know him?

EMMA

Good as I ever did. I don't mean to say we passed time
together—we were nothing but babies—but I used to see
him sometime at church, and at Sunday-school picnics
he generally wound up eating with us—my mother had
the freest hand on earth; the Mustians were *close*. So I
mostly saw him eating Mama's pie or cake—he was crazy
for sweets. (*Reaches for the picture, studies it; continues
half-privately, almost to herself*) Funny thing is, this is
how I see him, whenever I see him—looking like this,
so young and serious, not like he got to be. (*Stands with
the picture and walks to* ROSA's *window, continues
quietly but to* ROSA *again*) If he would have stayed this

way, Rosacoke, he'd be here this minute, helping us all. But he started to change. People have to change—I well know that—but he didn't have a dead leaf's will-power; so time did the changing on him, every step: and every step was down. He didn't have a thing he controlled but his looks—and you can't spend looks, can't feed them to children, can't go on begging people's pardon for hurts just because you look the way he did then. Still I never asked for anything else—not in 1930. Then when money got scarce as hen's back teeth, and his drunks commenced coming so close together they were one long drunk, and he was sleeping nights wherever he dropped in fields or by the road—I took it all like a bluefaced fool: it was take it or jump down the well and die. I never asked him to change a thing till it was too late, and he had filled me up with four big babies and himself to the eyes with bootleg liquor and then walked into a pickup truck going fifty miles an hour like it was a bed. But like I say, I don't recall him that way and I'm thankful. (*Rubs the picture on her apron to dust it; then walks to the mantel, props it there by one of* WESLEY) I'll leave it here so you can see it—be yours someday anyhow. None of the others would want it. (*Turns, studies* ROSA) Rosa, I've pressed some old baby clothes. Get up and take them to Mildred's baby please.

ROSACOKE

Mama, let me rest.

EMMA

Rest isn't what you need. You need to get up and live your life among people that love you—that have proved they love you for long years, Rosa. (*No reply from* ROSA, *reclining again*) Did the letter upset you?

ROSACOKE

No.

EMMA

How is he doing?

ROSACOKE

He never says that.

EMMA

What does he say?

ROSACOKE

(*Waits*) That he might come down some weekend soon if I make up my mind to tell him to and meet him halfway.

EMMA

Where would that be?—Courtland?

ROSACOKE

You know where it would be.

EMMA

Then tell him to step in the ocean and cool. And you stop waiting.

ROSACOKE

He isn't what I'm waiting for.

EMMA

Don't lie to me. What else is there but Judgment Day?

ROSACOKE

My whole life ahead. I mean to have a life.

EMMA

Then get up and start it—

ROSA *half-sits, mouth working silently.* MILO *runs in—porch, stairs—throws open* ROSA's *door.*

MILO

Cares are ended!

EMMA

Milo, go easy. Sissie's expecting.

MILO

So am I, Mama. Rosa, that little airplane landed on purpose. Guess who was in it? (*Rushes to answer himself*) —Willie Duke Aycock and a rich boyfriend that owns the plane!

ROSACOKE

Tell the truth

MILO

Bible truth. I stopped at the store to get Sim to help me in case of a crash; and before we could leave, the telephone rang—Willie's Mama called to ask for oysters: Willie's new friend wants oysters for supper. She said the family hadn't calmed down yet; said when that airplane touched ground in the pasture, every tit on the cow stood out like potlegs and streamed good milk!

ROSA *stands and turns to* EMMA.

ROSACOKE
I'll take those clothes on down to Mary's.

MILO
Stay where you are and start grinning wide.

ROSACOKE
Milo, what do you mean?

MILO
I mean what I said—your cares are ended. If Willie marries that fool with the plane, doesn't it mean you can walk right to Wesley—no briars in the path?

ROSACOKE
You ask Wesley that.

MILO
You ask him—shortly. Wesley came home in that airplane too.

EMMA *sits on the bed, looks to* ROSA. ROSA *stands before her mirror, puts a comb to her hair—slowly, not rushed.*

ROSACOKE
Is that the truth?

MILO

(*Raising a hand*) It's what Mrs. Aycock said on the phone.

ROSA *combs on slowly;* EMMA *rises.*

EMMA

I'll put those clothes in a bag for you, Rosa.

MILO

She's not moving, Mama. The clothes can wait. (*Moves to the open door, beckons* EMMA *to precede him. She does reluctantly.* MILO *follows her out*)

Alone, ROSA *puts down her comb; moves to the mantel, studies her father's picture briefly. Then she quietly moves downstairs to the empty porch; waits on the steps, watching the road. Shifts of light show the coming of evening. A few cars pass; none stops. She shivers as a fall chill rises, holds herself close. Behind her in the downstairs room all gather at the table for supper.* EMMA *turns on a lamp at the foot of the stairs and moves to the porch.*

EMMA

Rosa, come eat something.

ROSACOKE

Thank you, I couldn't.

The family eat silently behind her awhile; then EMMA *whispers to* BABY SISTER, *who moves out to* ROSA, *a sweater in hand.*

BABY SISTER

Mama sent you this.

ROSACOKE

Thank her for me. (*Puts it on carefully—not looking at*
BABY SISTER, *who waits behind*)

BABY SISTER

Someday will you explain it?

ROSACOKE

What?

BABY SISTER

What all this is for—why everybody punishes themselves like this.

ROSACOKE

You'll learn soon enough. (*Smiles*) Then explain it to
me. Don't worry; you'll learn.

BABY SISTER

You could leave here, Rosa—get a job in Raleigh.

ROSACOKE

(*Thinks*) I could. Every worry I've got travels light as
a tent though; I can pitch them anywhere.(BABY SISTER
stares on, shivering) You're turning blue—go in; save
your life. Might as well have one woman carry on the
name.

BABY SISTER

Women don't do that.

ROSACOKE

(*Nods, strokes her own shoulder*) It's the one thing they don't carry *here*. Get warm.

BABY SISTER *goes in.* ROSA *buttons the sweater, the lights and sound of a car approach, a car door slams.* WILLIE *and* HEYWOOD BETTS *enter quickly.*

WILLIE

Rosa, meet my aviator—Rosacoke Mustian this is Heywood Betts, my boyfriend that flew me down.

ROSACOKE

(*Smiles*) How do you do?

HEYWOOD

I've dislocated my neck, I think, but otherwise working —flying's just a hobby; scrap metal's my line.

ROSACOKE

Well, good luck in it. (*Retreats a step*) And good luck, Willie. (*Gives a small half-wave, then thinks herself rude*) Come in if you can.

HEYWOOD

I doubt I can. I'm being displayed to the family tonight —little showings all up and down this road.

WILLIE

Thank you but we're stopping by Marise's. (*Waits*) I thought you'd be with Wesley.

ROSACOKE

No.

HEYWOOD

Maybe he's laid up from our pasture landing.

WILLIE

Shoot, nothing bothers Wesley that much—does it, Rosa?

ROSACOKE

No, not much.

HEYWOOD

He looked plenty bothered this afternoon when you talked me into landing in your front yard.

WILLIE

Nothing bothers Wesley. He's just not himself. (*She strains up and kisses* HEYWOOD *on the ear*) In case I don't see you tomorrow, Rosa, goodbye. The three of us are flying back early tomorrow. Heywood's buying a World-War I submarine—

HEYWOOD

For the scrap—

WILLIE

I'm locking you in it and drowning the key. (*She moves off quickly*)

ROSACOKE

Goodbye. (*Looks toward the house, then moves to it slowly. The family are still in the dining room, beyond* ROSA'S *hearing*)

MILO

Yeah, but what right has she got to keep everybody she knows upset just because she fell for some poor rascal seven years ago but can't pin him down?

EMMA

She's got the right of being your sister.

BABY SISTER

Sissie, what songs did they sing at your wedding? I forgot.

MILO

Her Mama sang "Hallelujah!"—several verses.

SISSIE *shakes her head, disgusted.*

BABY SISTER

When I get married I want "Kiss of Fire" and then "Because."

MILO

Because of what?—you said just now nobody could pay you to marry a man. (*Toward the end of that,* ROSA *has entered and gone to the far wall to get the bag of clothes*) Where you been?

ROSACOKE

Walking.

MILO

Where you going now?

ROSACOKE

To take these clothes to Mildred's baby.

MILO

Won't me and Sissie need them?

ROSACOKE

Twenty-year-old rags?—here, keep them. Sure.

MILO

No, but you don't need to go to Mary's either—near dark and chilly.

ROSACOKE

When did you ever know anything I needed? (*Moves to leave*)

MILO

(*Lets her reach the front door, then calls behind her*) I know you need a good dose of Sissie's method. Sissie, tell Rosa what your old uncle said was the way to hold Milo.

SISSIE

I got you honest. My uncle never told me a word.

MILO

Yes he did. (ROSA *has waited in fascinated revulsion by the door.* MILO *advances on her, stands stiff in parody of a child's recitation, grins, and sings*)
"Pull up your petticoat, pull down your drawers, Give him a look at old Santy Claus."

EMMA *and* SISSIE *cry* "Milo!" *together.* BABY SISTER *laughs.* MILO *gives a schoolboy's bow to* ROSA, *who watches another moment; then leaves.*

2

A quarter-hour later, MARY SUTTON's *house. A room that seems empty—a chair, a table; on the table a wooden peach crate sits waiting.* ROSA *probes the emptiness by calling.*

ROSACOKE

Mary? Mary, I've brought Mildred's baby some clothes. (*No sign of* MARY. ROSA *stands puzzled in the door, then seems to hear a sound from the peach crate, goes there. As she sets down the bag and bends to see, the baby cries. She lifts him to calm him, but the crying increases so she puts him back*) Baby, I'm not what you need. (*Moves a step to leave. The door is blocked by* MARY. ROSA *points behind to the howling child*) Come on, Mary, and help this child.

MARY

(*Unsmiling*) What you done to Mildred's baby?

ROSACOKE

Not a thing—he's sick.

MARY

He ain't sick. He just passing time.

ROSACOKE

I came in to bring him these clothes and he woke up.

MARY

And you picked him up when I done just fed him?

ROSACOKE

I was trying to stop his crying, Mary. Don't get mad.
(*The crying is weaker.* MARY *enters and touches the
baby. He quiets*)

MARY

What you so scared of crying for? He come here crying
and he be crying when I ain't here to hush him. He got
his right to cry, Rosacoke; and why ain't you used to
babies by now?

ROSACOKE

I will be soon. Milo's wife is overdue.

MARY

(*Smiles at last*) Yes'm. Sit down, Miss Rosa. Thank
you for the clothes.

ROSACOKE

It's nearly night, Mary. I better get home.

MARY

You come by yourself?

ROSACOKE

Just me and my thoughts. (*Smiles*) I'll come back soon
and stay longer then.

MARY

Yes'm. I know you're busy tonight. They tell me Mr.
Wesley got him a plane.

ROSACOKE

News moves round here. No, that's not his plane. He
just hitched a ride.

MARY

How's he coming on, Rosacoke?

ROSACOKE

Wesley?—fine, I guess. I haven't laid eyes on him since
the funeral.

MARY

I didn't know that.

ROSACOKE

It's God's own truth. He's working in Norfolk, scarcer
than ever. Says I got to say do I really want him. I
thought I'd said it. (*Smiles with difficulty, meaning to
leave; moves to the door*) Mary, what must I do?

MARY

Don't ask me—here I sit alone.

ROSACOKE

But say anyhow—everybody else has.

MARY

(*Waits*) He what you need? (ROSA *seems to nod*) Hold him then, if you can. All I know. (MARY *points through the door*) He's right in yonder behind them trees.

ROSACOKE

(*Faces* MARY *another moment*) Mary, excuse me.

MARY

Step along, Rosacoke, or night'll catch you.

ROSA *leaves.*

3

A quarter-hour later, the porch of WESLEY's *home. He
sits on the top step, playing his harmonica, both hands
cupped round his mouth.* ROSA *enters carefully, un-
noticed by him, and stops five yards from the steps to
listen. He sees her and pauses.*

ROSACOKE

Don't stop. (*He plays on a little, the song unfinished*)
Is that all you know?

WESLEY

No. Oh no. (*Smiles*) But it's all I'm giving. Got to
save my strength.

ROSACOKE

(*Tries for lightness*) For what?

WESLEY

My life. (*Waits, smiles again*) My pitiful life.

ROSACOKE

I heard you playing almost to Mary's. (*Points behind*)
I've been to Mary's to see Mildred's baby. (WESLEY

laughs gently. It whines through his harp) If you managed everything good as you manage a harp, wouldn't none of your friends ever be upset.

WESLEY

Wesley's friends got to take Wesley—lock, stock, and block—or leave him alone.

ROSACOKE

Doesn't make his friends' life easy, does it?

WESLEY

(*Still smiling*) Who did I beg to be my friend?

ROSACOKE

You've spent your life—or the last seven years—drawing people to you.

WESLEY

They don't have to come. I don't carry a gun.

ROSACOKE

That may well be. (*Looks up to the sky—a night sky now*) Can I use your phone? It's darker than I counted on.

WESLEY

To get home, you mean? I can carry you.

ROSACOKE

Can you? I wonder.

WESLEY

I've wondered myself.

ROSACOKE

Reached any conclusions? (WESLEY *faces her plainly but does not speak*) Then while you're waiting, do me a favor—say "Rosacoke."

WESLEY

Why?

ROSACOKE

A gift to me.

WESLEY

Rosacoke.

ROSACOKE

Thank you. That's my name. Bet you haven't said it since late July.

WESLEY

(*Smiles*) I don't talk to trees and shrubs like some people if that's what you mean.

ROSACOKE

It's not what I mean. You're Wesley—is that still right?

WESLEY

Unless the law has changed it and not notified me.

ROSACOKE

Just checking. I know such a few facts about you that sometimes I wonder if I even know your name.

WESLEY

Yes ma'm. Rest easy. It's Wesley all right and is Wesley
walking you home or not?

ROSACOKE

I'd thank you—yes.

WESLEY

And you'd be welcome. (*Reaches behind on the porch,
finds a flashlight, descends toward her*) Won't cost you
a cent. (*Offers his hand, she takes it; they leave. Slowly
they walk through changes of light—time and place. In
dark spots,* WESLEY *does not use the flashlight and
makes no sound,* ROSA *stops at last*)

ROSACOKE

Might as well be on the motorcycle for all we've said.

WESLEY

What you want to say?

ROSACOKE

(*Waits*) I want to say you are half this trouble, that
you've never talked to me, and now you're gone, and
I don't know— (*Breaks off, shamed, in her old ha-
rangue*) I want to say I've said it *all*, till my teeth ache
with shame.

WESLEY

You haven't—not all. I've answered every question the
best I could, best *I* could. There's one left for you—
(*A sudden crashing in the near woods halts them*)
Jesus, Rosa!

ROSACOKE

Wesley!

As the sound retreats, they wait a stunned moment.

WESLEY

(*Half-whispers*) All my life I waited on that—

ROSACOKE

A deer? Me and Mildred saw one years ago.

WESLEY

A grown buck leading two does to water. They were killed all through here before you were born.

ROSACOKE

What water, Wesley?

WESLEY

Mr. Isaac's spring. I've seen tracks there. I scared them, talking.

ROSACOKE

Will he try again?

WESLEY

If he doesn't hear us.

ROSACOKE

We could wait.

WESLEY

You want to?

ROSA *thinks a moment, nods. They sit on a low rise and silently wait. Then the deer cross toward the spring— delicate sounds.* WESLEY *watches closely;* ROSA *watches him. A moment to realize they are gone; then* WESLEY *moves to stand.* ROSA *touches his arm.*

ROSACOKE

Since it's not too cold, we could walk behind them— find the spring.

WESLEY

If you want to. We won't see the deer.

ROSACOKE

If we went gently— (WESLEY *studies her, takes her hand, and rises. Slowly—together, silent—they move inward. Deeper darkness.* ROSA *at last pulls back on his hand*) Listen.

WESLEY

To what?

ROSACOKE

I thought we might hear them. Mildred and I saw the deer we saw in a field like this.

WESLEY

Not this field.

ROSACOKE

How do you know?

WESLEY

(*His voice begins to alter in speed and pitch till it gradually seems a stranger's*) This is my private field. Mr. Isaac doesn't know he owns this field. Nobody knows this field but me.

ROSACOKE

I never knew it.

WESLEY

You know it now.

ROSACOKE

I know it now. (*They stand, hands joined, but she cannot see him. She begins to feel fear but tries to speak lightly*) It's night all right—dark early now. Wesley, switch on your light. I can't see you. (*She moves away*)

WESLEY

(*Waits*) You mean to take pictures?

ROSACOKE

No.

WESLEY

Then if you don't need light, this boy doesn't.

He offers a hand, firm but undemanding. She stands a moment, then goes to accept it. He sets both hands on her shoulders and presses her down. On their knees in near-darkness, they kiss—hands at sides. Then ROSA *begins to unbutton his shirt.* WESLEY *waits till she's finished—his chest bare to her; she lays a palm on it. He takes her wrist, pushes her gently to her back. In deeper dark, he opens his belt; slides down his pants and trousers, begins to bare* ROSA. *Then he lies upon her and slowly moves. Total dark till* WESLEY *can speak.*

WESLEY

Thank you, Lady. (*He slowly rolls off, lies on his back beside her, and launches a flashlight beam on the sky*) Did you know this light won't ever stop flying? Nothing to block it. Millions of years from tonight—somewhere —people in space will move in my light.

ROSACOKE

Is that something else you learned in the Navy?

WESLEY

Ain't I a good learner? (*He reaches to touch* ROSA *again. She seizes his wrist and holds him back*) Why?

ROSACOKE

I got to go home.

WESLEY

What you got at home as good as what's here? (*Takes her hand, pulls it down toward himself.* ROSA *draws back and stands*)

ROSACOKE

If you won't carry me, I'll gladly walk; but since you know these woods so well, please lend me your light.

WESLEY

(*Sits upright, throws his light on her face, sees the baffling change*) Are you all right?

ROSACOKE

I'm all right. (*Moves to leave*)

WESLEY stands and puts his clothes together, then comes up behind her, shines his light at the ground.

WESLEY

You need to remember—the way you feel is a natural thing after what we've done. You answered me. The sadness'll pass. You'll feel good as you ever did. Gradually better. (*Touches her shoulder; she doesn't turn*)

ROSACOKE

We haven't done nothing. I haven't answered nothing. (*Moves on again to the bottom porch-step of the Mustian house. The porch light is on. At last she turns*)

WESLEY

I'm out of my depth. Hell, Rosa, I'm drowning. Stand still and say what you want out of me.

ROSACOKE

I don't want anything you've got to give. I've just been mistaken

SISSIE

(*Inside*) Help me, Milo. Help me please.

Light rises in the upstairs room—now MILO and SISSIE's: SISSIE in bed, MILO, EMMA, MARY SUTTON, and DR. SLEDGE silently busy round her.

ROSACOKE

Sissie's started. Please leave. (*Climbs two steps*)

WESLEY

Are you all right?

ROSACOKE

I answered that once. I was just mistaken. If that's *you*, Wesley; if that's what you've been, I've been wrong for years.

WESLEY

(*Waits, nods twice*) It's me *and* you.

ROSA *shakes her head No, looks to the house, then quickly enters.* WESLEY *stands a moment, then moves away. A long moan from* SISSIE. ROSA *has climbed the stairs and stands in the open door.*

MILO

Thank God you're here.

Three shouts from SISSIE. ROSA *watches for a long hard moment, then turns, comes quickly down and out the front door.*

EMMA

Mary, see about Rosacoke.

MARY *follows* ROSA, *stops in the front door.*

MARY

(*Harshly*) Rosa! (ROSA *stops in the yard*) Where you running now? That girl's in trouble.

ROSACOKE

Who is she to me?

MARY

I thought you and Milo were brother and sister. It's his wife, Rosacoke—the one he picked—and whatever baby comes here tonight will be his and part yours. So where're you running?

ROSACOKE

I can't go back in that room, Mary. I'm no use there.

MARY

Then wait in the kitchen. Baby Sister's in there with Mildred's baby and Mr. Macey Cupton. They're making candy. It's going to be a long setting-up, I can tell you. Her waters've broke and she's dry as a bone.

ROSACOKE

(*Moves toward the house*) I need to talk to you.

MARY

About what?

ROSACOKE

I did what you said.

MARY

I never said what to do, I asked you a question. (*A new cry from* SISSIE. MARY *turns toward the door*) I'll come down to see you if they give me a chance.

ROSA *nods and follows* MARY *in. The dining room lights* —BABY SISTER *and* MACEY GUPTON *at the table.* BABY SISTER *reaches for fudge from a platter as* ROSA *enters.*

ROSACOKE

Baby Sister, one sick woman is enough.

MACEY

Don't grudge her something harmless as fudge. Four
years ago Marise hadn't thought about much but candy.
Look at her now—got three babies out of me quick as
gunshots and a fourth on the way. (A *moan from* SISSIE,
exhausted now) Sounds like she's dying, I know. She's
not. She's doing what's as natural as skin. Some
women do it easier than that. Marise has them easy as
puppies—drops one, stands up, spreads the bed, and
cooks my supper in one afternoon.

ROSACOKE

(*Not rudely*) Macey, go home.

MACEY

Milo called me here. No, Marise is strong. She said to
me "Stop"; said to me right after Frederick was born,
"Macey, let's stop—let's rest awhile." I told her,
"Marise, I've wanted a house full of children from you
since the day I saw you walking to the store with an
empty Coke bottle."

ROSACOKE

Wanted them for what? (*Macey turns to her, baffled*)
Baby Sister, look at what time it is.

BABY SISTER

O.K., I've looked.

ROSACOKE

Then go on to bed. You've got Sunday school tomorrow.

BABY SISTER

You're not my boss. I'm waiting for the baby.

MACEY

Go to bed, Honey. There'll be regular babies in this house now.

ROSACOKE

Macey, we're tired.

MARY *enters quickly, a slip of paper in her hand.*

MARY

Doctor says get this medicine, Mr. Macey.

MACEY

(*Studies the prescription*) Hope the druggist can read this—dozens of years of education and writes like a chicken. Thank God I'm a fool. (*Takes his coat and leaves*)

ROSA *looks to* MARY *but* MARY *has moved to the peach crate on the floor and squats by that—*MILDRED'S *baby. So* ROSA *goes to* BABY SISTER.

ROSACOKE

(*Half whispers*) The baby's awake. Now go to bed.

BABY SISTER

(*Strains to see him*) What's his name?

ROSACOKE

Go on, Baby Sister. (BABY SISTER *goes.* ROSA *moves to where* MARY *is arranging the baby's blanket*) Mary, what is his name?

MARY

I call him Sledge after Dr. Sledge that tried to save Mildred, but I don't know—I expect his name's Ransom. Sammy Ransom hasn't mentioned feeding him though. (*Stands, moves to the table, sits.* ROSA *remains beside the baby*) I ain't blaming Sammy. Mildred didn't know his name herself—at least, she never told me.

ROSACOKE

She didn't know. I met her in the road last February. We hadn't seen each other since summer; and we stood there saying how cold it was till it seemed we didn't have another word to say. So we said goodbye and Mildred moved and her coat swung open and there was this little new belly riding on her. I said "Mildred, what's that?"' She said "Nothing but a baby." I said "Whose?" and she said, "Several asked me not to say." I said "Is anybody marrying you?" She said, "No hurry. Just so he come here *named*." I said "Are you glad?" She said, "*Glad* ain't got nothing to do with it, Rosa. He coming here whether I'm glad or not." (*Stands slowly, moves to the table near* MARY) Once she was gone round the bend in the road, she was gone for good. Never saw her again—not alive, not her face.

MARY

(*Studies* ROSA) Why are you telling me that? Mildred done what she had to do. Don't blame her now.

ROSACOKE

(*Rousing from memory*) Not blaming, just remembering. I've got a good memory.

MARY

Noticed you have. (*Waits*) Rosacoke, you got to live in the present.

ROSACOKE

I've been trying to—tonight. That doesn't stop me regretting Mildred—that she stretched out in the dark somewhere and took this baby from some hot boy that didn't love her, that she didn't love no more than a snake.

MARY

How old are you, child?—nearly Mildred's age, ain't you? And you still thinking and talking about *love*, still waiting round for love to strike? Time's running out on you, Rosacoke. Time's coming soon when you got to rinse your eyes and see that most people lie down and *die* without love, not the love you're talking about —two people bowing and scraping to themselves for forty years with grins on their mouths. Of course Mildred didn't love nobody like that. But she knew what she needed and took it—and it killed her. That was her hard luck. You asked me this evening what to do with Mr. Wesley; and I said if he's what you need, then hold him.

ROSACOKE

I tried that, just now. (*Points behind*) What if that shows you were wrong for years?

MARY

Wrong about what?

ROSACOKE

Who somebody was.

MARY

Then you take who they are or kill them and run.
(*Smiles*)

MILO

(*Runs in*) Where the hell is Macey?

MARY

Gone for the medicine.

MILO

We need it now. Both of them are dying. Rosa, come
on with me. We'll have to go get it. (ROSA *looks to her
hands, does not rise.* MILO *moves to the door*) You owe
me this much.

ROSACOKE

You ought to have thought of that three hours ago
when you sang me your song.

MILO *waits a moment, then leaves.*

MARY

That was somebody needed you. Who're you going to
have left?

ROSA *stands and runs out.* MILO *is halfway across the
yard.*

ROSACOKE

I beg your pardon.

MILO

Come on.

ROSA *follows* MILO *toward the car.* EMMA *comes to the front door.*

EMMA

Rosa— (MILO *stops in his tracks, his back to the house.* ROSA *moves back to* EMMA) It never breathed.

ROSACOKE

What was it?

EMMA

A boy. (*Looks to* MILO, *his back still turned*) God help me to tell him.

ROSACOKE

You'll freeze. I'll go to Milo.

EMMA

And stick beside him, whatever he does? You promise me that?

ROSACOKE

Yes'm. I will.

EMMA

Tell him Sissie's safe.

*ROSA nods and goes toward MILO, stops six feet away.
He slightly turns.*

ROSACOKE

It's over. Milo—he never even breathed.

MILO

He? Don't you know his name? He's had a name since the day I made him.

ROSACOKE

Father's name?

MILO

(*Nods*) That was the trouble—that and the sorry mother he had. Sissie killed him sure as if she cut him with a knife—to punish me.

ROSACOKE

Milo, that isn't so. I won't stand here and say I love Sissie, but she worked nine months to make that child, and nobody works that long in hate.

MILO

I've worked every day of my life in hate.

ROSACOKE

(*Still six feet away*) Milo, take that back. You don't mean that. (*He looks to the ground but never says No; so ROSA goes to him, encircles him from behind, lays her head against him, talks from there*) I'll help you any way I can, any way you need. (*Waits, no reply*) We could take a ride. Or a walk up the road. It's not

that cold. When you were a boy, let you be worried,
you'd walk for miles—remember that? (*No reply.* MILO
looks to the house) Let's walk to Mr. Isaac's and back.
That's what we need.

MILO *stares on at the house, then gently walks from*
ROSA'S *arms toward the porch, stops four steps away.*

MILO

What I need to do and got to do are two different
things. But thank you, Rosa.

ROSA *stands awhile—exhausted, abandoned. Then she
slowly enters the silent house, climbs to her room,
removes her sweater, walks to the window, stares at the
night. Her face is blank; she holds herself and shudders
slightly.*

ACT THREE

1

The Mustian dining room, noon, a Sunday in late December. BABY SISTER *stands at the window;* SISSIE *behind her is setting the table. In her dim room above,* ROSA *stands ironing.*

SISSIE

All this family does is wait. Waiting can kill you; I know. Know well. Come here and help me, Baby Sister.

BABY SISTER

(*Waits, then patiently explains*) Sissie, Rato's our brother that we haven't seen for nine long months—so nobody's waiting idle today and nobody's dying.

SISSIE

Rosacoke is dying—or going to die if she goes on shut up in that cold room another month like she's done this past. Ironing, *ironing*—you'd think she was running an orphanage, all the ironing she does. How come she can't do it down here with the humans?

BABY SISTER

He's here! (*Runs to the foot of the stairs, calls up*)
Mama! Rosa! Rato is home! (*Runs to the yard and
waves at the distance*)

EMMA

(*Enters from the back of the house, takes a sweater
from a hook at the foot of the stairs, calls up*) Rosa?
(*No reply*) Rosa, Rato is home. (*Looks into the room
where* SISSIE *still putters*) Rato is home.

SISSIE

Heard he was. Won't Rosa come down?

EMMA

Rosa is a grown woman. I don't know. (*As* EMMA
reaches the yard, RATO *and* MILO *appear—*RATO *in a
wrinkled uniform,* MILO *carrying his duffle.* EMMA *stops
short of* RATO) Welcome home, Son. Are you feeling
good? (*Opens her arms but* RATO *looks past her to*
ROSA'S *window—*ROSA *stands looking down, grave like*
MILO. EMMA *touches* RATO'S *shoulders to brush him off,
strains up to kiss his neck*) You're feeling fine. You've
put on weight.

RATO

Army food. Rosa sick? (*No response. He looks to all
the faces*) Sick with what?

EMMA

She's all right—just the Christmas dumps.

BABY SISTER

(*Quickly to* RATO) Everybody tells me I'm too young, but I know Rosa is not herself—comes home from work, climbs to her room, lies there staring, or washes and irons clothes she washed the night before. She hasn't even eaten since Friday night.

EMMA

No, I took her something. (*Takes* RATO's *arm*) You'll cheer her up.

RATO

I'll help anybody if they tell me what's wrong. (*Looks up again.* ROSA *gives a little wave, half-beckoning; then goes back to ironing*)

MILO

(*Gently*) You try it. Everybody else has lost.

They all go in. RATO *climbs at once to* ROSA'S, *opens without knocking, stands on the sill.*

ROSACOKE

(*In place*) Merry Christmas, Rato.

RATO

(*Moves to her, holds out his hand to touch.* ROSA *takes it a moment*) Merry Christmas yourself. What you doing up here?

ROSACOKE

(*Smiles at last, shrugs*) I live up here.

RATO

(*Looks round the too-neat room—the only disorder, a pile of rough laundry on the bed*) You taking in wash?

ROSACOKE

(*Shutting the door behind them*) No, I just seem to use a lot of clothes.

RATO

Ought to join the Army—just have the one suit of clothes on your back.

ROSACOKE

(*Laughing*) Rato, that's not so.

RATO

(*Nods, walks to* ROSA's *mantel, studies the picture of their father, then reaches beside it and takes up a picture that is laid face-down*) You ought to get a new one—he's changed so much. (*Shows her the large tenth-grade picture of* WESLEY)

ROSACOKE

(*Moves to the ironing board*) I don't think so.

RATO

He has though. (*Replaces the picture*) Rosa, when are your plans?

ROSACOKE

There aren't any plans.

RATO

You and Wesley, I mean.

ROSACOKE

(*Trying for lightness*) The morning after Judgment Day. 'There aren't any plans.

RATO

I thought you had him. (ROSA *wants to answer fully but can only shake her head. Both stand steady, hands at their sides*) You told me years ago he'd be your life. We were back in the woods—Milo had left us. You asked me what was a happy life; and I said, "For people to let me alone"; but you said your idea was marrying Wesley and having some children that would look like him and have his name but be half yours and answer when you call—and for that to last as long as you lasted. You forgot that? (ROSA *shakes her head*) Don't forget it. It's all in the world you know how to do. The *world's* solid fools. I'm the one in this family that's traveled so listen to me.

ROSA *faces him but cannot reply.*

BABY SISTER

(*From the foot of the stairs*) Rato, dinner is ready.

RATO

(*Half-whispers*) Dinner is ready.

ROSACOKE

I can't eat a mouthful.

RATO

I've eaten just peanuts since Friday—come on. (*She shakes her head*) What's wrong with you?

ROSACOKE

I've got Wesley's baby.

RATO

Good. (*She shakes her head*) Why not? Does Wesley
know?

ROSACOKE

I don't want Wesley.

RATO

Why?

ROSACOKE

He doesn't want me.

RATO

You don't know that. You're hard on people, Rosa.
We're not as quick as you. Tell him now and wait till
he answers.

*Through that, the family has gathered in the dining
room.* BABY SISTER *calls again.*

BABY SISTER

Rato—

RATO

Tell him. (*Offers his hand*) And come on with me. I've
worked to see you. You're the one here I like.

ROSA *thinks, half-smiles, takes his hand, and they go.
In the dining room, all quickly sit at the table and bow
for grace.*

EMMA

Lord, make us thankful for Your many blessings. (*All mutter "Amen," begin to pass dishes*) Son, do you have a chaplain for the Baptists or does everybody get the same one?

RATO

Haven't seen a Baptist since early April. Just Catholics.

EMMA

You'll see some tonight.

RATO

Where?

BABY SISTER

The church—we're having the Christmas pageant and you're in it.

RATO

No I'm not.

MILO

Yes you are. Me and you're Wise Men.

RATO

Are you in it, Rosa?

ROSACOKE

No, I was Mary last year—remember?

RATO

If you're not, I'm not.

MILO

Yes you are. I'm the head Wise Man. You're my helper.

BABY SISTER

Who's the third?

Embarrassed silence. ROSA *stands, takes the empty biscuit plate, and speaks to* RATO.

ROSACOKE

The third one is Wesley, if he comes in time. (*Moves to the kitchen*)

EMMA

(*Whispers to* MILO) Is Wesley here yet?

MILO

(*Still chewing, face down*) He's here. I saw him when I went to get Rato.

EMMA

What did he say?

MILO

He said was he welcome in this house still?

EMMA

What did you say?

MILO

Mama, Rosacoke is not my business. (*Waits*) I said "What do you mean?" Wesley said he had written to her three times since that weekend in early November—

even asked her to visit him in Norfolk at Thanksgiving
—but he hadn't heard a word.

EMMA

What did you say to that?

MILO

I said, "You're no more confused than us. Rosa lives
above us—takes up bed space, breathes the same air—
but for three weeks now, she's a stranger to us.

EMMA

Did you tell him he was still welcome though?

MILO

I don't think he is—not with her, not now. Anyhow,
I've given my last advice. Nothing I said ever helped
anybody.

ROSA *reappears from the kitchen with a heaped plate of
biscuits and goes to serve* RATO.

RATO

When is Christmas?

ROSACOKE

Wednesday. (*Goes to her chair*)

EMMA

You anxious, Son?

RATO *suddenly stands, rushes to the foot of the stairs,
finds his duffle, brings it in, and squats to search it.*

BABY SISTER

Did you bring your gun?

RATO

No, I brought everybody presents from the P.X. Everything's cheap there.

EMMA

That's fine, Son, but wait till Wednesday.

RATO

No ma'm. We all could be sick by Wednesday.

He finds a few boxes tied with ribbon, weighs them in his hand; gives one to BABY SISTER, *who opens it quickly —and brandishes a baby-toy: a large elephant. She is plainly embarrassed.*

BABY SISTER

Thank you, Rato.

RATO

(*Still squatting*) That's O.K.

EMMA

That's nice, Sister. That can be your mascot.

RATO

(*Stands, sees the elephant, seizes it back*) This wasn't yours. I got it mixed-up (SISSIE'*s face clenches but she tries to hold on. Silent pain is visible on all*) Listen. I bought all this back before Thanksgiving. I'll have to check it. I forgot what's what.

SISSIE *rises carefully and leaves.* RATO *watches her, puzzled.*

EMMA

Sit down, Son, and finish your dinner. Christmas is coming; everybody's just tired.

RATO

Amen to that.

MILO

(*Quietly*) Hallelujah, Amen.

2

A quarter-hour later, the Mustian dining room. ROSA *and* EMMA *clear the table quietly. A distant car passes.*

EMMA

Whose car was that?

ROSACOKE

Macey Gupton's.

EMMA

Headed to church? (ROSA *nods.* EMMA *glances to a clock on the mantel)* Lord, it's time for pageant practice and Macey's beating me.

ROSACOKE

Getting Marise there in plenty of time.

EMMA

Marise isn't Mary after all—didn't I tell you? She stopped me yesterday morning at the store and said she just felt too big now but that she knew Willie would gladly fill in. I knew it too but I waited as late as I could for you. Then when you didn't feel any better this morning, I tried to reach Willie. (*She has roused no sign of interest in* ROSA *but continues nervously*) Her mother said Willie and Heywood had gone for a little ride—at nine in the morning—but that she knew Willie would be proud to serve. So Willie gets her chance after all these years—maybe God will forgive me before I die! Frederick Gupton is Jesus and I hope he's tired enough to shut up tonight. (*The sound of another car.* ROSA *moves toward the window to see.* EMMA *waits a moment, comes up behind her, reaches to touch her shoulder but doesn't*) Rosacoke, you're my smartest child; and I've never claimed to understand you, but I know one thing—we're well into winter and you've barely laughed since summer ended. I know some reasons but I doubt I know all; and even if you are mine, I won't ask anything you don't need to tell. I just want to say, if you've got any kind of trouble needs telling—I'm your mother at least. Nobody else is. (ROSA *does not turn*) If there's anybody you don't want to see at the pageant tonight, stay at home; I won't make you go. I understand. (ROSA *slowly shakes her head No*) What does that mean?

ROSACOKE

(*Facing the road*) That you don't understand.

EMMA

Tell me then. Now.

ROSACOKE

You said you wouldn't ask.

EMMA

I lied. I'm asking.

ROSACOKE

(*Turning, tired but calm*) I'll tell you when I get home from work tomorrow.

EMMA

You don't know for sure?

ROSACOKE

I know, yes ma'm.

EMMA

Is there somebody you need to tell before me?

ROSACOKE

I halfway thought so. As usual he's absent.

EMMA

He's not. He's a half-mile away—a few bare trees.

ROSACOKE

That's the moon to me.

EMMA

Then you put him there. He's one local boy. Let me speak to him now; I'll see him at practice.

ROSACOKE

Do and I'll die. This is my thing, Mama.

EMMA

Yours and one other human's, if I understand.

ROSACOKE

You don't understand.

EMMA

It's not the first time. Will I tomorrow evening?

ROSACOKE

You'll know tomorrow evening.

EMMA

(*Stands a long moment, unable to touch her*) I've got to go now. (*Moves to the door*) Why don't you fix up and walk to Mr. Isaac's?—take him his Christmas candy early. You've carried candy to him every Christmas since your father died.

ROSACOKE

(*Nods Yes but speaks to the window*) I know my duties.

EMMA

I'm praying you do. (*Leaves slowly,* ROSA *still at the window*)

ROSA *stays in place a moment, then moves to the foot of the stairs; takes her coat, a paper sack tied with green ribbon; walks out and slowly to* MR. ISAAC ALSTON'S *door; knocks three times.* SAMMY *comes in clean work clothes. At first he seems not to recognize her.*

SAMMY

Rosacoke. I didn't know you. How're you getting on?

ROSACOKE

Kicking—but not high, Sammy.

SAMMY

I hope you improve by Christmas. Step in.

ROSACOKE

No, I'll head on back. But I won't be going to church this evening, so I brought Mr. Isaac his Christmas candy. (*Offers the sack*)

SAMMY

(*Reaches to take it, then draws back*) You give it to him. He needs some company.

ROSACOKE

What he'll need is rest if he's going to the pageant.

SAMMY

(*Gestures inward*) He don't do nothing but rest, Rosacoke. It's near about all he lives for now—horehound candy and going to ride and company. You be his company this afternoon.

ROSA *enters with* SAMMY. *They move to a room where* MR. ISAAC *sits in a chair, neatly dressed—no tie but his collar buttoned at the neck. He is chewing slowly.* SAMMY *goes to him, sits him up straighter.*

SAMMY

This is your friend, Rosacoke, Mr. Isaac. Tell her Merry Christmas.

MR. ISAAC

(*Stares at her closely*) Merry Christmas. (*He chews some white mass*)

SAMMY

What in the world you eating now? (*Presses* MR. ISAAC'S *lower jaw down, coaxes him gently*) Spit it out, Mr. Isaac—that ain't candy; that's soap. (MR. ISAAC *spits the mass into* SAMMY'S *palm*) Now you sit here and talk to Rosacoke while I get you something to rinse your mouth else you'll be blowing bubbles at the Christmas pageant. Sit here, Miss Rosa. (*Draws a straight chair close to* MR. ISAAC'S. ROSA *comes to it, stands*) There's a lot worse things than dying, Rosacoke. How's Miss Sissie?

ROSACOKE

She's out of bed now. Her mind's still tender.

SAMMY

Wasn't it a boy? What was his name?

ROSACOKE

It would've been Horatio, after our father.

SAMMY

I hope they get them a new one soon.

ROSACOKE

I don't know if they could stand it again.

SAMMY

People not having much luck this year. (*Waits*) Have you seen Mildred's baby?

ROSACOKE

Yes, more than once.

SAMMY

Don't he take after Mildred? I saw him last week. Miss Mary had him at the church, don't you know; and I seen him—first time.

ROSACOKE

Sammy, I better go—

SAMMY

Please sit with him while I get some water. Give him his candy. (ROSA *nods,* SAMMY *goes*)

ROSACOKE

(*Sits, pulls the ribbon off the sack, offers it open*) Merry Christmas, Mr. Isaac—and many more.

MR. ISAAC

(*His good hand enters the sack*) I will. I can't dic. If you were to shoot me, I wouldn't die.

ROSACOKE

I won't shoot you then.

MR. ISAAC *loudly crushes one piece of candy, chews it slowly.* ROSA *moves to rise. With shocking speed, his good hand takes her wrist and presses her down. Then he studies her hand.*

MR. ISAAC

Who are you?

ROSACOKE

I'm Rosacoke—Horatio and Emma Mustian's girl.
You've known me all my life.

MR. ISAAC

Are the children here?

ROSACOKE

No, Mr. Isaac. I'm as single as you.

MR. ISAAC

Why?

ROSACOKE

(*Trying for lightness*) Why are you?

MR. ISAAC

(*Releases her hand*) Nobody ever asked me to change.
(*Smiles, his mouth full of candy*)

ROSACOKE

(*Half-smiling*) That's most people's reason.

MR. ISAAC

And most people live and die in misery. (*Chews on
awhile*) I do not understand.

ROSACOKE

Well, don't ask me. I'm twenty. (*Waits, then hopes to
change the drift*) I hear you're going to church this
evening.

MR. ISAAC

(*Nods*) I go every time they open the door but I don't pray. If I can't die, how come I should pray? (*Points to a spot on the bare floor*) I don't pray no more than that dog does yonder.

Held by his force, ROSA *follows the point for a moment; then rises.*

ROSACOKE

I better be—

MR. ISAAC

I'll give you a nickle to scratch my head.

ROSACOKE

(*Sees a brush*) I'll brush it for you.

She sets the sack of candy in his lap, takes the brush, stands behind him, and begins to brush with short timid strokes. Then as she eases into the job, he seems to doze. ROSA *pauses then and stares out his window, more nearly at peace than for six weeks past.*

MR. ISAAC

(*Eyes still shut, not moving beneath her hand*) Tell me who you are. I'll remember you.

ROSACOKE

I'm one of Emma Mustian's children that you've been seeing for twenty years—passing in the road or back in the woods at your spring or at church—so if you don't know by now, it must not be your fault. (*At that,*

WESLEY *knocks on* MR. ISAAC's *front door.* SAMMY *goes; they exchange an inaudible greeting. Then* SAMMY *waves him in, and they move toward* MR. ISAAC's *room as* ROSA *continues*) I've changed till I hardly know myself. Been changed by a boy I thought I wanted—

SAMMY

I got *you* a present, Rosacoke.

WESLEY

(*Tentatively*) Merry Christmas, Rosa.

ROSACOKE

(*Surfaces slowly from reverie*) Why have you trailed me?

WESLEY

Your mother sent me home to get you. Sissie said you were here. Willie's eloped with Heywood Betts, and you've got to be in the pageant tonight, so they need you to practice.

ROSACOKE

No. (*She strains at control but intends to leave; she takes two steps round* MR. ISAAC's *chair. He claws at her coat. She stops to listen. He urgently holds the sack of candy toward her*)

MR. ISAAC

Give this to the children.

ROSA *stares at the candy in baffled fear.*

SAMMY

(*Leans to* MR. ISAAC, *tries to take the candy*) What children, Mr. Isaac? This is Rosacoke and that's your candy, your Christmas present.

MR. ISAAC

(*Clutches the candy, still offers it to* ROSA) This is for the children. Say it's from me. They were good to me.

ROSA *shakes her head slowly as if a paralysis were flooding her. Then she gives a low groan and runs from the room—out the front door,* WESLEY *a few strides behind her. At the edge of the yard, he touches her shoulder. She stops there, beyond him.*

WESLEY

Please tell me what hurts you.

ROSACOKE

Nothing you can cure.

WESLEY

You don't know that. *I* don't know that till you tell me the trouble.

ROSACOKE

It's *my* trouble and if you don't know by now—

WESLEY

I don't know anything about you, Rosa; and I've known you seven years. Six weeks ago you welcomed me, then turned yourself like a weapon against me—won't answer my letters, won't tell me nothing. You don't have the right. (*With both hands he takes her arms at the elbows, holds her firmly but gently*) We've got to go practice. Everybody's waiting. Come on with me. (ROSA *shakes her head No*) Rosa, Willie has gone. You've got to take her part or your mother's show will fail.

ROSACOKE

Marise Gupton can do it.

WESLEY

You haven't seen Marise lately then. She's the size of that house. (*Points behind him, glances back.* SAMMY *stands in the door.* WESLEY *waves him in*) It's all right, Sammy. (SAMMY *nods and goes*)

ROSACOKE

It's not all right.

WESLEY

(*Still behind her, he reaches for her left hand. She lets him hold it*) Why?

ROSACOKE

(*Frees her hand; turns to face him, calm but tired*) Marise Gupton is not the only person working on a child.

WESLEY

Who do you mean?

ROSACOKE

I mean Rosacoke.

WESLEY

(*Thinks a long moment*) And Wesley then. (ROSA *shakes her head No, not fiercely but firmly. With his hand in the air, he asks her to wait*) Understand this one thing and answer—you don't know nobody but me, do you?

ROSACOKE

I don't know you.

WESLEY

Don't lie to me—you know what's here. (*Waits*) You don't know anybody else, do you, Rosa?

ROSACOKE

You know I don't.

WESLEY

(*Draws one long breath, slowly exhales it; makes no try to touch her again but extends his offer in a mild half-whisper*) Come on then. We got to go practice. (*He turns to go and has gone four steps before he knows he is walking alone. Stops and half-turns.* ROSA *is facing her home but has not moved.* WESLEY *comes back to her; by now his voice is almost happy*) Rosa, why didn't you tell me sooner?

ROSACOKE

What good would that have done?

WESLEY

Good?—maybe not. But it would've been fair.

ROSACOKE

I can't see I owe you two more words.

WESLEY

Try one. Try *Wesley*. Wesley's my name.

ROSACOKE

(*Smiles*) I'll try to remember that. (*Takes a homeward step, turns*) *Weapons*, Wesley—I have lain down and got up and worked through years with you driven into my chest like a nail.

WESLEY *takes that, full-face; then slowly comes toward her, begins quietly as if to himself.*

WESLEY

Rosa, you aren't the only human made out of skin. What do you think us others are? What do you think I've been these long years?—asbestos? wood? I'm not, not now if I ever was. I may not have talked as well as you. Or planned as far. I may have disappointed you hundreds of times, but I'm still the person you claimed to love and plan a life on. I've shied from plans. (*Waits*) I'm not shying now. We'll leave here after the pageant tonight and be in South Carolina by day— we won't need a license; that's where everybody goes. We can spend a night somewhere, be back by Christmas eve—

ROSACOKE

I'm not everybody. I'm just the cause of this one baby. It's mine—something really mine from the start; I'll have it on my own.

WESLEY

And shame your mother and feed it how and tell it
what? Not a hundred percent yours, it's not. Remember
that along with my name. (ROSA *watches him closely
but doesn't answer*) Do something about me. Tell me
"Go" or "Stay." (*Silence still*) We can live. I've paid
up all my debts; every penny I make from here on is
mine.

ROSACOKE

(*Genuinely thinking aloud*) Let me get this straight.
You offer to drive me to South Carolina and marry me
at dawn in some poor justice of the peace's living room,
then give me a little one-day vacation and bring me
home for Christmas with my family that will be cut
again by this second blow, then take me on to Norfolk
to spend my life shut in two rented rooms while you
sell motorcycles—me waiting out my baby, sick and
alone, eating what we could afford and pressing your
shirts and staring out a window in my spare time at
concrete roads and people that look like they hate
each other. —That's what you're standing here, offering
me, after all these years?

WESLEY

Yes. It was all I ever had to offer. I never said I was
anything but Wesley. All the rest you made up yourself
and hung on me. Sure, that's one way of seeing my
plan; but if everybody looked at their chances like
that, people would have gone out of style long ago.

ROSACOKE

Maybe they should've.

WESLEY

You don't mean that.

ROSACOKE

I think I do. I haven't been sleeping.

WESLEY

You're talking like the old Wesley now.

ROSACOKE

You said there was just one Wesley all along.

WESLEY

(*Shakes his head slightly*) There's Wesley's you never dreamed of, Rosa.

ROSACOKE

(*Opens her mouth to answer, finds only a kernel of what seems knowledge*) That may be so. But—look— I'm free. I'm standing here seeing you and, Wesley, I'm free.

WESLEY

You're wrong. And I'm sorry. We've got till tonight. Believe I'm serious—whatever it means weeks or years from now—and tell me tonight. (ROSA *starts to answer*) Please. Tonight.

As ROSA *faces him—silent, not moving—a piano begins to play "Joy to the World." After six bars* ROSA *moves toward the sound;* WESLEY *follows. When the light has dimmed,* BABY SISTER—*hidden—sings the whole first stanza.*

BABY SISTER

"Joy to the world! The Lord is come!
Let earth receive her king;
Let every heart prepare Him room,
And heaven and nature sing."

3

The same night, Delight Church. Low light on BABY
SISTER *dressed as an angel, completing the song, ". . .
and nature sing." She stands above a huddle of adolescent shepherds. Then we see* ROSA *as Mary at the
manger,* MACEY GUPTON *as Joseph behind her. Dark at
one side,* MR. ISAAC *in his chair with* SAMMY *beside him.
On the other side a choir, not robed, consisting of*
EMMA, SISSIE, MARISE GUPTON, *and others.*

MR. VEREEN

(*Unseen*) "Now when Jesus was born in Bethlehem
of Judaea in the days of Herod the King, behold, there
came Wise Men from the east to Jerusalem, saying—"

RATO

(*Unseen at the back*) "Where is he that is born King
of the Jews?"

MILO

(*Unseen*) "For we have seen his star in the east—"

WESLEY

(*Unseen, a pause*) "And are come to worship him."

Piano plays a brief introduction; then all the Wise Men sing together, dark at the back.

WISE MEN

"We three Kings of Orient are.
Bearing gifts we traverse afar,
Field and fountain, moor and mountain,
Following yonder star."

ROSA *is staring closely at the manger—*FREDERICK GUP-TON. *The choir joins the Wise Men for each refrain.*

WISE MEN AND CHOIR

"O star of wonder, star of night,
Star with royal beauty bright,
Westward leading, still proceeding,
Guide us to thy perfect light."

RATO *moves forward with long slow steps in time to his solo verse.* ROSA *watches him closely.*

RATO

"Born a babe on Bethlehem's plain,
Gold I bring to crown Him again,
King forever, ceasing never
Over us all to reign."

As the choir, MILO, *and* WESLEY *sing the refrain,* RATO *reaches the manger and—no flicker of recognition to* ROSA, *though his eyes fix on her—kneels to present his gift: a brass bowl. Then he stands aside.*

CHOIR, MILO, WESLEY

"O star of wonder, star of night,
Star with royal beauty bright,
Westward leading, still proceeding,
Guide us to thy perfect light."

MILO *moves forward, faster than his own verse; slows only as he kneels, presents his gift (a small wood chest), and sees the baby. His face clouds painfully.* ROSA *watches through the refrain.*

MILO

"Frankincense to offer have I;
Incense owns a Deity nigh.
Prayer and praising all men raising,
Worship Him, God on high."

CHOIR AND WESLEY

"O star of wonder, star of night,
Star with royal beauty bright,
Westward leading, still proceeding,
Guide us to thy perfect light."

MILO *stands aside with* RATO, *and* WESLEY *moves forward.*

WESLEY

"Myrrh is mine. Its bitter perfume
Breathes a life of gathering gloom—
Sorrowing, sighing, bleeding, dying,
Sealed in the stone-cold tomb."

CHOIR, RATO, MILO

"O star of wonder, star of night,
Star with royal beauty bright,
Westward leading, still proceeding,
Guide us to thy perfect light."

As the choir begins the last refrain, WESLEY *kneels with
his gift—a glass butter dish. He meets* ROSA'S *eyes for a
moment at first; but* FREDERICK *whimpers, then begins
to cry, and* ROSA *looks to him.* MACEY *leans from behind her, whispers to lift him. As* WESLEY *rises to join
the other Wise Men,* ROSA *lifts* FREDERICK *and holds
him through the rest. Her growing decision is firmed
by two things—*FREDERICK *in her arms and the strange
familiar face of* WESLEY, *her choice from the faces of
all her life, as he kneels a second time when the Wise
Men leave.*

MR. VEREEN

(*Unseen*) "Mary kept all these things and pondered
them in her heart. And the shepherds returned, glorify-
ing and praising God for all the things that they had
heard and seen. . . . The Wise Men, warned of God
in a dream that they should not return to Herod, departed into their own country another way. And when
they were departed, behold, the angel of the Lord
appeareth to Joseph in a dream, saying—"

BABY SISTER

(*To* MACEY) "Arise, and take the young child and his
mother, and flee into Egypt and be thou there until
I bring thee word."

MACEY *helps* ROSA *to stand in place with* FREDERICK.
*The piano briefly introduces "Silent Night." The choir
sings the necessary verses while the recessional proceeds
—shepherds bowing in a group to* ROSA; RATO *and* MILO
separately and slower, WESLEY *last. He fixes on* ROSA'S
*face but cannot catch her eye. She is deep in her part
still, studying* FREDERICK. WESLEY *rises and leaves—no
sign of emotion. The choir files off in increasing dark—
one light remains on* ROSA *and* FREDERICK, MACEY *dark
behind them.* ROSA *faces out now, firm and clear, but
shows no answer.*

CHOIR

"Silent night, holy night—
All is calm, all is bright
Round yon Virgin Mother and Child,
Holy Infant so tender and mild.
Sleep in heavenly peace,
Sleep in heavenly peace."

4

A quarter hour later, Delight churchyard. MARISE GUP-
TON *comes out of the church in a winter coat—a cold
night. She holds* FREDERICK *closely and speaks to him
frankly as to an adult.*

MARISE

You did all right. Jesus cried more than once, in my
Bible anyhow.

ROSA *comes out, approaches* MARISE.

ROSACOKE

He did fine, didn't he?

MARISE

He did all right.

ROSACOKE

I thought I'd scared him that one time though.

MARISE

(*To* FREDERICK) He may've had a bad dream. He still
dreams a lot.

MACEY *comes out, joins them, speaks to* FREDERICK *gently.*

MACEY
You all but ruined it—Rosa handled you though.
(*Looks up*) Thank you, Rosa. (*Smiles*) Want to take
him for Christmas? We could use some relief.

ROSACOKE
(*Smiles also*) So could I, Macey. My hands are full—

MACEY
Most people's are. (*Puts his arm round* MARISE *to lead
her off*) Well, Merry Christmas. (ROSA *nods*) Tell
Rosacoke "Merry Christmas," Marise.

MARISE
(*Looking up vaguely, finding* ROSA'S *face*) We'll be
thinking of you, Rosa.

As the GUPTONS *leave,* WESLEY *comes out—suit and tie—
and faces* ROSA *across a wide gap. They are gravely silent,
looking still.* EMMA, BABY SISTER, RATO, MILO, *and* SISSIE
come out. EMMA *steps forward slightly, looks a moment.*

EMMA
Rosacoke, are you coming with us?

ROSA *looks to* WESLEY. *He turns to* EMMA.

WESLEY
I can carry her.

EMMA

You promise?

WESLEY

Promise.

EMMA

You've failed me before.

WESLEY

I may again. But not this time.

EMMA

(*Waits, then nods, half-waves*) Be careful. Merry Christmas. (*Turns slowly to leave*)

ROSACOKE

(*In place but suddenly*) That's Wednesday. Wait till Wednesday—

EMMA waits a moment, nods, gives her little wave again, and goes. RATO, BABY SISTER, MILO, *and* SISSIE *follow quietly—only* RATO *and* SISSIE *waving. To their vanishing backs,* ROSA *gives one broad gesture—farewell, gentle banishment—ending at her mouth: an instant of grief.*

WESLEY

(*In place*) I can carry you. (*His hand comes slightly up, offered not extended*)

ROSACOKE

Why should you want to?

WESLEY *does not speak but his hand stays out, his calm gaze holds.* ROSA *studies him a moment—face and hand —then goes to him. Separate, a step apart, they leave together.*

REYNOLDS PRICE

Born in Macon, North Carolina in 1933, Reynolds Price attended North Carolina schools and received his Bachelor of Arts degree from Duke University. As a Rhodes Scholar he studied for three years at Merton College, Oxford, receiving the Bachelor of Letters. In 1958 he returned to Duke where he teaches for one term each year in the Department of English. There he began and completed A Long and Happy Life, *which was published in 1962 and received the award of the William Faulkner Foundation for a notable first novel. In 1961 he again traveled to England where he worked for a year at the stories which were published in 1963 as* The Names and Faces of Heroes. *His second novel* A Generous Man *appeared in 1966; his third* Love and Work, *in 1968; his fourth* The Surface of Earth, *in 1975; his second volume of stories* Permanent Errors, *in 1970. In the same year his fiction received an Award in Literature from The American Academy and The National Institute of Arts and Letters. The citation read, "His gifts are a vigorous intelligence, a strongly individual perception of the nature—both physical and psychological—of a given time and place, of the variety in kind and intensity of human relationships. Over all his prose fiction there is a poet's daring and control." His collection of essays and scenes* Things Themselves *was published in 1972.*

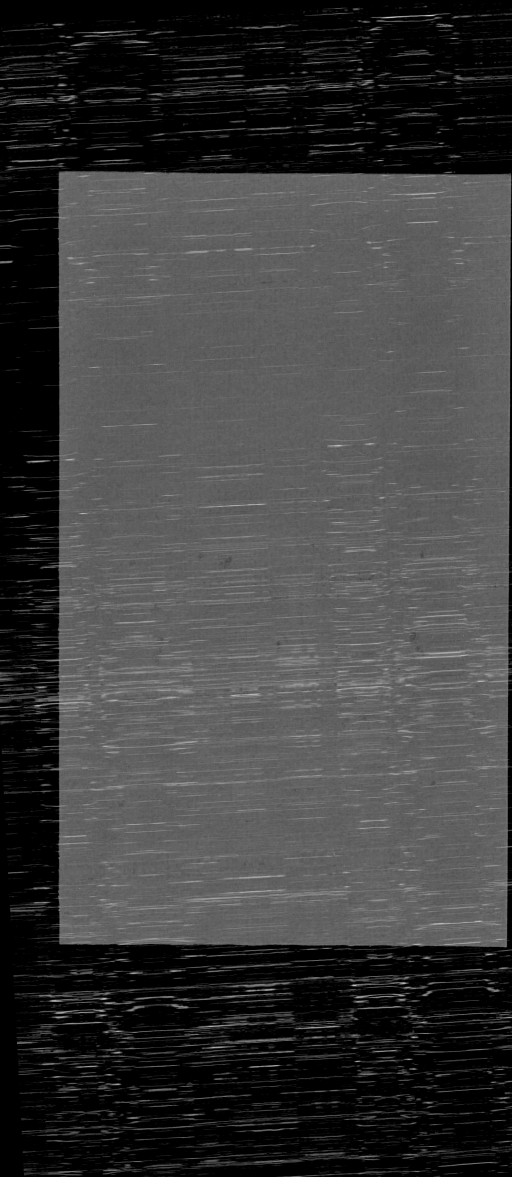